SAVING HISTORIC ROADS

MERCER PARK ROAD, OMAHA, NEBRASKA, 1926.
Bostwick-Fronhardt Collection, Western Heritage Museum.

SAVING HISTORIC ROADS

DESIGN AND POLICY GUIDELINES

PAUL DANIEL MARRIOTT
THE NATIONAL TRUST
FOR HISTORIC PRESERVATION

Preservation Press

JOHN WILEY & SONS, INC.

NEW YORK / CHICHESTER / WEINHEIM / BRISBANE / TORONTO / SINGAPORE

A cooperative publication with the National Trust for Historic Preservation, Washington, D.C., chartered by Congress in 1949 to encourage the preservation of sites, buildings, and communities significant in American history and culture.

This text is printed on acid-free paper.

This publication is designed to provide accurate and authoritative information in regard to the subject matter covered. It is sold with the understanding that the publisher is not engaged in rendering legal, accounting, or other professional services. If legal advice or other expert assistance is required, the services of a competent professional person should be sought.

Library of Congress Cataloging-in-Publication Data

Marriott, Paul Daniel.
Saving historic roads : design and policy guidelines / Paul Daniel Marriott.
p. cm.
Includes bibliographical references and index.
ISBN 0-471-19762-9 (cloth : alk. paper)
1. Roads—United States—Design and construction—History.
2. Roads—United States—Maintenance and repair.
3. Historic preservation—United States—Planning. I. Title.
TE23.M37 1997   97-14443
363.6'9—dc21

Printed in the United States of America

10 9 8 7 6 5 4 3 2 1

FOR
THE BRONX RIVER PARKWAY

CONTENTS

ACKNOWLEDGMENTS

This book was developed, in part, through a generous grant from the Marpat Foundation. Additional support was provided by the James A. Macdonald Foundation. I am especially indebted to Shelley Mastran, Ph.D., without whose sincere commitment this book would not have been possible.

The following individuals contributed immensely of their time and talent:

Carol Ahlgren
John F. Byrne
Carlos Luis Caceras
Betsy Cuthbertson
Eric DeLony
Bruce Eberle
Elizabeth Fischer
Eliot Foulds
Richard E. Greenwood, Ph.D.
Diane Kane, Ph.D.
Robert McCullough

Elizabeth Merritt
MaryAnn Naber
Laura Nelson
Sally Pearce
Beth Savage
Fred Skaer
Amy Steiner
Peter Szabo
Andrea Tingey
Raymond L. Towne

Grateful acknowledgment is made to the following organizations for their assistance and interest: the National Park Service, Historic American Engineering Record, Natchez Trace Parkway, Olmsted Center for Landscape Preservation; the Federal Highway Administration; the American Association of State Highway and Transportation Officials (AASHTO); the California Department of Transportation (Caltrans); the Connecticut Department of Transportation; Nebraska State Historical Society; the Lincoln Highway Association; the Snickersville Turnpike Association; Oregon Department of Transportation; the National Trust for Historic Preservation, Rural Heritage Program, Law and Policy Department; Chicago Park District; Metropolitan District Commission, Boston; University of Hawaii; the Westchester County (New York) Archives; Historic Route 66 Federation; Westchester County (New York) Department of Planning; Library of Congress, Prints and Photographs Division.

THE NATIONAL
TASK FORCE FOR
HISTORICAL ROADS

The National Task Force for Historic Roads (NTFHR) is housed within the Rural Heritage Program at the National Trust for Historic Preservation in Washington, D.C. The NTFHR is an ad hoc organization inviting the comment and participation of all individuals interested in historic roads.

The purpose of the NTFHR is to promote the recognition of historic roads—aesthetic, engineered, and cultural, as well as routes of historic significance—in the United States and to advocate the protection of their integrity of design, purpose, and use in a manner that is both historically appropriate and responsive to modern safety needs.

The NTFHR's position is that concerns for appropriate safety standards and historic resources need not be mutually exclusive. The NTFHR recognizes that the provision of a safe driving environment is of paramount importance and, as such, will not advocate the use of lesser safety standards for historic roads. Rather, the NTFHR will advocate the use of standards (existing, modified, or new) sensitive to historic roads. Additionally, the NTFHR shall look at alternate methods (environmental, psychological) by which physical safety can be enhanced.

AUTHOR'S NOTE

This book began in 1993, quite accidentally, with a request to prepare a minor paper outlining the issues and threats facing the Bronx River Parkway in New York. What began as a focused study of one parkway rapidly escalated to encompass larger national influences affecting the Bronx River and other historic parkways around the United States. The focus on parkways became exclusionary within weeks as historic boulevards and early transcontinental highways, among others, began surfacing with similar concerns. The overwhelming concern was *how to manage the preservation of historic road resources in the face of the engineering, legal, and social realities of the late twentieth century.*

The minor paper became a major one, and soon a policy paper was presented to the civil engineering community at an AASHTO meeting in 1994. Before long, The National Task Force for Historic Roads was established, a conference planned, and I found myself the unexpected recipient of historic road inquiries and eventually this book offer.

Over these past four years of research, I have received scores of telephone calls from preservationists across the United States expressing concern, frustration, and helplessness regarding the preservation of their historic roads. I have been heartened by success stories and saddened by the loss of all too many miles of pavement. Vivid descriptions of leafy motor roads carved through the mountains and frenetic freeways weaving among art deco skyscrapers, have reminded me how much historic roads embody our cultural and designed landscapes.

Saving Historic Roads is the first publication dedicated to the preservation of historic roads. It is the result of a personal journey through a previously unexplored world of civil engineering and the law. It has also been a physical journey across the nation from the colonial roads of New England to the Alaska Highway. And it has been a journey back to the summer hills and winter shadows of the National Road of my childhood in Maryland. It is my hope that this book will inspire the creative energy and fervent commitment needed to save the historic roads each of us remembers.

The preservation of historic roads is a new and legitimate field within the world of historic preservation. It is a movement whose time has arrived. Resource age, recent loss, and a growing appreciation for our automobile legacy have converged as we approach a new century and as yet undreamed modes of moving ourselves about the planet.

Despite the euphoria surrounding a new movement, real problems and real losses do threaten many of our historic roads. The Bronx River Parkway, where this all began for me, is still not secure despite all its pastoral magnificence and planning brilliance. Let us hope that we as a society have learned the lesson of preservation, and that our historic roads need not be sacrificed to the irresponsible decisions and policies that enabled the loss of Penn Station, scarcely fourteen miles away from the Bronx River Parkway, to the shortsightedness of perceived transportation needs in the 1960s.

THE CASSELMAN RIVER BRIDGE, NATIONAL ROAD, GARRETT COUNTY, MARYLAND. WHEN OPENED IN 1817 IT WAS THE LARGEST MASONARY ARCH BRIDGE CONSTRUCTED IN THE UNITED STATES.
Daniel Paul Marriott, Dorothy Altice.

SAVING HISTORIC ROADS

SPEER BOULEVARD, DENVER, COLORADO.
The Denver Public Library, Western History Collection.

Chapter 1
INTRODUCTION

∼ *Purpose*

The purpose of this book is to assist you in the identification and preservation of historic roads. Such roads, designed and constructed in the past but still in use today, represent some of the most difficult resources to preserve. Therefore, this book is designed to familiarize you with the many issues surrounding historic roads, introduce you to the language of engineering and highway design, and identify the different strategies currently available for the preservation of historic roads.

Our historic roads are in danger. Across the United States these historic resources are being lost at an alarming rate. Whether the proposed straightening of a parkway, the removal of ancient trees shading a country lane, or the destruction of remaining sections of early transcontinental highways, our historic roads are at a critical point in time. In 1995, Iowa lost a portion of the Lincoln Highway, New York State rebuilt the Saw Mill River Parkway, and Yellowstone National Park rebuilt many miles of historic park roads. Due to severe threats to the historic integrity of the Bronx River Parkway—the first modern motor parkway—the National Trust for Historic Preservation listed it on the 1995 list of "America's Eleven Most Endangered Historic Places." A combination of resource age, ignorance, increased traffic, and a litigious society has placed heavy burdens on these significant transportation resources.

This country has a rich history of roadway development. From early overland routes such as the Boston Post Road in New England and El Camino Reals (Spanish Royal Ways) in California, Texas, and New Mexico to the National Road, the first federally funded interstate in 1806 (the first section between Cumberland, Maryland, and

THE BRONX RIVER PARKWAY (1906–1924) BEGAN AS AN EFFORT TO CLEAN UP THE
FOULED BRONX RIVER IN WESTCHESTER COUNTY, N.Y. SHANTIES AND PRIVIES
ALONG THE RIVER WERE DOCUMENTED IN 1912 PRIOR TO CONSTRUCTION.
Courtesy of the Westchester (N.Y.) County Archives.

IN ADDITION TO ENVIRONMENTAL PROBLEMS, THE BRONX RIVER PARKWAY
COMMISSION SOUGHT TO ADDRESS SERIOUS AESTHETIC CONCERNS WITHIN THE
BRONX RIVER VALLEY—1913.
Courtesy of the Westchester (N.Y.) County Archives.

BY 1922 THE BRONX RIVER PARKWAY BECAME THE PRINCIPAL LEISURE AND RECREATION SPINE IN WESTCHESTER COUNTY. IT ALSO OPENED THE COUNTY'S GREEN HILLS FOR NEW SUBURBAN DEVELOPMENT FROM NEW YORK CITY. THE PARKWAY WAS SUCH A SUCCESS, IT INSPIRED A PARKWAY SYSTEM LINKING ALL OF WESTCHESTER COUNTY.
Courtesy of the Westchester (N.Y.) County Archives.

Wheeling, West Virginia, opened in 1818) and the innovative parkways and park roads of the early twentieth century, we have been striving in ever creative ways to link our people, resources, and communities. Whether country lanes, urban boulevards, or prototypical freeways, historic roads represent a part of a precious legacy of the opening up of a continent. Their innovations represent a constant striving for improvement, and their aesthetic sensibilities a response to the diverse regions and traditions of the United States.

The adequate preservation of historic roads involves more than an appreciation for history. Historic roads constitute one of the most difficult resources to preserve. By their nature, they generally traverse great distances and include a broader contextual landscape. The ability to preserve, maintain, and protect the integrity of the corridor through which they travel is important. They represent a resource that, in many instances, is still functioning as originally designed.

They are a misunderstood resource—how can something still in use be historic?

As the preservation movement matures, the time has come to address historic resources not traditionally recognized. In a nation whose very fabric was defined by transportation initiatives, a focus on historic roads is needed to preserve significant road resources before they are lost forever.

Horizontal Alignment Is Not About Your TV

As you learn more about historic roads in your community, you will quickly become aware of the fact that roads and roadway management techniques carry a distinct vocabulary not familiar to most preservationists. What is horizontal alignment? What is a vertical curve? A clear zone? This book will teach you a new language to enable you to both understand and speak the transportation jargon when advocating the preservation of a historic road. Here's a sampling to get you started:

Alignment. The way in which a road moves across the landscape; its curves, straight sections, and hills; more technically, the precise engineering formulas that lay out a road.

Horizontal alignment. The movement to the left or right of the roadway (its curves).

Vertical alignment. The movement up and down of the roadway (its hills).

Clear zone. A recommended area alongside a roadway clear of all potential road hazards (something a car might strike) such as trees, rocks, utility poles, and the like.

Sight distance. The length of the road ahead that is visible to the driver. A driver approaching an intersection at the crest of a hill, for example, would have a limited sight distance due to the fact that he or she could not easily see cars approaching from the opposite side of the hill.

This book will make you aware of the options that are currently available for the preservation of historic roads. Happily, there are many creative methods—some of which are illustrated in case studies in this book—by which historic roads can be preserved. Knowing these options and being able to share them with your community and your road manager will assist you greatly.

Remember, most transportation departments and agencies have little experience with historic roads. Their primary mission is the safe and efficient movement of traffic. Their preservation experience to date has most likely been associated with the impact of a road project on a nearby historic resource—a house, for example. The idea of addressing *the road* as historic is new. Therefore you cannot assume that the individuals involved with the day-to-day management, planning, and maintenance of your historic road will understand or recognize the distinctive alignments, engineering advancements, or famous designers associated with it.

HUNDREDS OF MAIN STREETS, SUCH AS MILITARY AVENUE (C. 1940) IN BENSON, NEBRASKA, ARE BEING FORCED TO SACRIFICE HISTORY AND PEDESTRIAN SCALE TO THE NEEDS OF THE MODERN AUTOMOBILE.
Historical Society of Douglas County Library/Archives Center, Omaha, NE.

How to Use This Book

Due to the diversity of historic roads, this book must necessarily address a broad range of information. Chapter 2 identifies the different types of historic roads; Chapter 3 examines the existing policies, programs, and issues you should be aware of; Chapter 4 provides an introduction to the Green Book—the central engineering reference most road decisions are based on. Chapters 5 and 6 help you apply this information to your historic road. Chapter 7 presents you with six case studies of historic road success stories.

The Management Entity

You will find frequent references to the *road management entity* or *road manager.* These references refer to the individuals or agencies responsible for making decisions regarding the historic road. In most instances this will be a single agency. In some situations more than one office or agency may be responsible for the road. In general, for most states, historic roads (and most roads) tend to be managed by the state department of transportation (DOT)—the management entity. For some historic roads, in some states, the management entity may be a local department of public works (DPW), a transportation agency, a park or recreation office, a highway authority, or a federal land manager (National Park Service, U.S. Forest Service, Bureau of Land Management, Bureau of Indian Affairs). References to the road management entity or the road manager in this book will apply to any of the above.

Questions About Your Historic Road

Before you begin, review the following 25 questions regarding your historic road. You may not be able to answer them with great confidence if at all—it doesn't matter. They have been designed to start you thinking about what you have and what you hope to accomplish with your historic road. These questions will be repeated in greater detail in Chapter 5 after you have had the opportunity to learn more about what historic roads are.

TWENTY-FIVE QUESTIONS

Defining your road
1. Is your road historic?
2. What type of historic road do you have? (From Chapter 2.)
3. How is the road managed?

4. What standards guide the management of the road?
5. What is the functional classification of the road?
6. Does the road have any current restrictions or prohibitions on its use?
7. What is the nature of the traffic on your historic road?
8. Who pays for maintenance and upkeep of the road?

Defining the issues facing your historic road

9. Are there threats to the integrity of your historic road?
10. If there are threats, how immediate are they?
11. Does the road have demonstrated safety problems?
12. If there have been previous alterations to the historic road for safety, have the changes enhanced the safety of the route?
13. Are existing local or state standards applied consistently?

Responding to specific proposed changes or threats

14. What policies are being cited regarding the proposed activity?
15. What are the accident statistics for the area in question?
16. Have there been any previous efforts to enhance preservation or safety due to similar issues?
17. What sections of the American Association of State Highway and Transportation Officials (AASHTO) Green Book, if any, are being referenced for this project? (See Chapter 4 for full title of this publication.)
18. What outside experts can offer you technical assistance or provide you with letters of support or documentation regarding your historic road?
19. Are federal or state funds being used for this project?
20. Has the required Environmental Impact Statement (EIS) or Environmental Assessment (EA) been prepared?

Defining an appropriate course of action

21. What do you hope to accomplish?
22. What specific actions will be needed to accomplish your goals?
23. What other key players are involved, directly or indirectly, in decisions regarding your historic road?
24. What resources do you have?
25. When is compromise acceptable and when is it not?

MANY ROADS IN THE UNITED STATES ARE KNOWN AND CHERISHED AS ICONS WITHIN OUR CULTURE. BROADWAY, PENNSYLVANIA AVENUE, CASTRO STREET, THE LAS VEGAS STRIP, AND BOURBON STREET ALL GENERATE STRONG NATIONAL IMAGES. *Paul Daniel Marriott.*

Don't Point the Finger of Blame

Many communities are quick to point the finger of blame at the engineering profession for the poor management or destruction of historic roads. While there are some engineers for which this is true, there are many instances in which the engineer's hands have been tied by policies and procedures dictated by state standards, safety, funding, or liability issues. Remember, the engineering profession is focused on the movement of traffic and the protection of human life. Before you point the finger of blame at the engineers (or any other professional for that matter) and risk losing a potential ally, make a few inquiries—who made the decision versus who is carrying it out? What precipitated the decision in the first place? Would your local engineer be sympathetic to your historic road if the community assisted his or her office in investigating available options supportive of your historic road?

THE OLD NATCHEZ TRACE, JEFFERSON COUNTY, MISSISSIPPI.
Natchez Trace Parkway, National Park Service.

Chapter 2
HISTORIC ROADS DEFINED

In general, historic roads are roads that, through design, experience, or association, have contributed to our culture in a meaningful way. The type of road, its history, and current condition will determine the most appropriate action for preservation.

The National Task Force for Historic Roads (NTFHR) has identified three types of historic roads: aesthetic routes, engineered routes, and cultural routes.

∽ Aesthetic Routes

Aesthetic routes represent historic roads for which the primary rationale for development was the design and provision of a specific visitor experience. Aesthetic routes such as parkways and park roads have historically been intensively designed and developed for the purpose of leisure, recreation, and commemoration. They have a documented origin and construction date. Never intended as the fastest or quickest route, such roads typically follow the natural topography of the region and are most often associated with a designed landscape or park space. In urban areas, park boulevards and monumental avenues exhibit an equally high level of detail and composition. Aesthetic routes are roads for which the alignment and details are key to the experience. Special materials, plantings, lighting, and even building facades contribute to the character of these roads. Alterations to any component of these roads (alignment, details, and affiliated landscape) will significantly impact the historic integrity of the resource.

LAKE SHORE DRIVE AT BELMONT HARBOR, C. 1945. CHICAGO'S WORLD-FAMOUS DRIVE IS A CAREFULLY PLANNED, DETAILED, AND DESIGNED AESTHETIC ROUTE. *Courtesy Chicago Park District, Special Collections.*

A CLASSIC AESTHETIC ROUTE, THE ENTRANGE ROAD AT YOSEMITE NATIONAL PARK IN CALIFORNIA, WAS CAREFULLY DESIGNED WITHIN THE NATURAL LANDSCAPE. *Paul Daniel Marriott.*

Examples of aesthetic routes include:
    The Bronx River Parkway, Westchester County, New York
    The Colonial Parkway, Virginia
    Monument Avenue, Richmond, Virginia
    The Chicago Boulevard system
    The Rockefeller Carriage Roads, Acadia National Park, Maine

⌁ *Engineered Routes*

Roads designed for a specific transportation goal, such as the movement of people, goods, and services, represent the largest category of roads. Engineered routes, like aesthetic routes, will have a documented origin or authorization and construction date. These are roads that may have been developed to open isolated areas to commerce, link the nation, or simply serve our communities—roads for

THE BUTT OF MANY JOKES, THE NEW JERSEY TURNPIKE NONETHELESS REPRESENTS
A SIGNIFICANT ADVANCE IN SAFE, HIGH-SPEED TRAVEL. THIS ENGINEERED ROUTE
WAS DESIGNED TO "REMOVE THE PRESENT HANDICAPS AND HAZARDS ON THE
CONGESTED HIGHWAYS IN THE STATE AND TO PROVIDE FOR THE CONSTRUCTION
OF MODERN EXPRESS HIGHWAYS EMBODYING EVERY KNOWN SAFETY DEVICE."
—NEW JERSEY TURNPIKE AUTHORITY ACT OF 1948.
From the collection of the author.

THE NATIONAL ROAD, THE FIRST FEDERALLY FUNDED HIGHWAY IN THE UNITED
STATES (1806) MADE ITS WAY TO CENTERVILLE, INDIANA, BY 1828. THIS ENGINEERED
ROUTE OPENED THE FARMS IN THE MIDWEST TO THE EASTERN SEABOARD.
Paul Daniel Marriott.

which the aesthetic experience was often secondary. Their alignment
and detail are important in their representation of technology and
culture. Most generally, for these resources, speed, safety, and economy determined the design. Due to location or remaining details,
however, many engineered routes have taken on aesthetic qualities
and associations. Many city grid patterns and our first transcontinental highways are typical of this category. Examples of engineered
routes include

> The Lincoln Highway, New York, New York, to San Francisco,
> California
> The National Road, Cumberland, Maryland, to Vandalia, Illinois
> U.S. Route 66, Chicago, Illinois, to Los Angeles, California
> The Alaska Highway, Fairbanks, Alaska, to Dawson Creek, British
> Columbia

A Historic Road?

The Pulaski Skyway in northern New Jersey is one of America's pioneer elevated expressways. Designed at a time when only 2% of America's roads were hard-surfaced all-weather roads, the soaring steel cantilevers of the Skyway are an engineering landmark. Completed in 1932 as a connection to the newly opened Holland Tunnel, a primary gateway for automotive traffic into Manhattan, the Pulaski Skyway was one of the first public roads designed specifically for high-speed automobile and commercial truck traffic.

The Pulaski Skyway is a significant milestone in U.S. transportation history. The Skyway was one of the first routes where a roadway was viewed as a conduit for moving large volumes of traffic. Up until this time, with the exception of a few parkways, limited access roadways were unknown. Principal commercial and transportation routes were frequently brought to a standstill as local traffic, through traffic, and adjacent property access all competed for the road. The opening of the Holland Tunnel in 1927 created intense traffic congestion overnight in Hoboken, New Jersey. Accordingly, the Skyway was elevated above the surrounding communities and landscape in order that traffic could flow free from the interference of cross streets, local traffic, and adjacent property access. While many communities today have been negatively impacted by elevated highways, we cannot overlook the innovation of the Pulaski Skyway and the industrial beauty of this powerful structure.

On March 8, 1996, the Pulaski Skyway was found eligible for listing in the National Register of Historic Places by the Deputy Historic Preservation Officer for New Jersey as part of the 6.25-mile U.S. Routes 1 and 9 Historic District.

PREPARED BY ANDREA TINGEY

THE PULASKI SKYWAY, NEW JERSEY.
Kinney E. Clark, New Jersey Historic Preservation Office.

～ *Cultural Routes*

Cultural routes represent roads that evolved through necessity or tradition. While these roads may have a documented date of origin, they were developed without the intensive engineering and design practices associated with aesthetic and engineered routes. These may be roads that evolved from Native American trails, colonial post roads, or simply from convenient connections between villages. Now in automobile use, cultural routes have generally undergone significant changes and modifications since their inception, often leading to multiple layers of development, providing interesting historical juxtapositions, and a challenge for preservationists. Generally the only original feature of these roads is the historic corridor through which they pass. Remaining roadside features such as churches and inns may give a clue to the history of the route—their spacing a clue to settlement and travel patterns. Remember, too, that road construction projects done at different times in the route's history may have left different layers of interesting historic resources.

THE FARM ROADS OF LANCASTER COUNTY, PENNSYLVANIA, EMBODY THE TRADITIONS AND PACE OF ANOTHER ERA. SUCH CULTURAL ROUTES ACROSS THE COUNTRY FACE PRESSURES TO MEET CONTEMPORARY ROADWAY GUIDELINES AND POLICIES.
Paul Daniel Marriott.

THE PALI ROAD ON OAHU, HAWAII, EVOLVED FROM A TRAIL PROVIDING THE ONLY
LINK TO THE NORTH SIDE OF THE ISLAND. IT WAS ON THIS ROAD THAT THE DECISIVE
BATTLE WAS FOUGHT TO UNITE THE HAWAIIAN ISLANDS UNDER A SINGLE KINGDOM.
KING KAMEHAMEHA, IN 1795, PUSHED THE OPPOSING TROOPS UP AND OVER THE
CLIFF (PALI). A CULTURAL ROUTE STILL EVOLVING, MODERN STATE ROUTE 61 HAS
REPLACED THIS SEGMENT, SEEN HERE C. 1941.
Courtesy the Bishop Museum, Honolulu, Hawaii.

Examples of cultural routes include
   The Boston Post Road, New York to Boston
   Ministerial Road, Rhode Island
   El Camino Real, California and Texas
   Pali Road, Hawaii
   River Road, Louisiana

⌒ *Multicategory Roads*

There may be instances in which a road fits into more than one category. Consider for example the Arroyo Seco Parkway in California.
The parkway was designed as both an engineered route and an aesthetic drive. In like manner, the Columbia River Highway was designed as a scenic route and a commercial route into the timber- and
grain-producing interior of the Cascade Range of Oregon. Therefore,
it has attributes of an aesthetic route and an engineered route. Whenever possible, if your road represents more than one category, try to de-

CROWN POINT ON THE COLUMBIA RIVER HIGHWAY, CONSTRUCTED IN 1916–1917,
CONTINUES TO IMPRESS VISITORS WITH ITS SPECTACULAR VIEWS OF THE COLUMBIA
RIVER GORGE.
Paul Daniel Marriott.

THE STREET PLAN OF WASHINGTON, D.C., DESIGNED BY PIERRE CHARLES L'ENFANT
IN 1791 AND SURVEYED BY ANDREW ELLICOTT AND BENJAMIN BANNEKER, HAS
BEEN NOMINATED TO THE NATIONAL REGISTER OF HISTORIC PLACES.
Paul Daniel Marriott.

termine if one is more significant than the other. Lastly, remember that the patterning of streets may be significant—for example, radiating avenues from Indianapolis' central circle or Savannah's street grid and squares established by James Oglethorpe in 1733.

Historic Road or Historic Trail?

Historic routes can be difficult to define. As a general rule of thumb, historic routes that function today in an automobile capacity will benefit from the information in this book. Many historic roads that began as trails continue to be utilized today—U.S. Route 1, for example. Historic routes that no longer serve a primary transportation function, such as historic trails like the Oregon Trail, face equally compelling but different threats. To address issues surrounding historic trails, you should contact:

National Park Service
Trails and Greenways Division of the National Center for Recreation and Conservation
PO Box 37127
Washington, DC 20013-7127

∽

It's All in a Name

Did you know that there are specific definitions for road name suffixes such as street, avenue, boulevard, and parkway? Seventeenth-century Bostonians knew this and deliberately labeled new thoroughfares as streets. *Why? Because by the late sixteenth century the term street had come to be regarded as an element of an urban area—a street being defined by architectural edges (buildings). Thus, through a name, the early Bostonians expressed their confidence in the future of the fledgling port by establishing sophisticated urban references to their meandering and muddy roads.*

Many people are unaware that there are still specific definitions for road name suffixes. For example, an avenue *is a broad thoroughfare, usually tree lined, and a* boulevard *is the same with a planted median area down the center. A* lane *is a narrow passage defined by buildings, hedges, or fences. A* parkway *is a road that is contiguous with or links park areas. Parkways must involve a recreational component in their truest definition.*

The next time you drive through a new residential subdivision or come across Corporate Boulevard or Industrial Parkway, ask yourself if the roads are properly named.

∽

THE ARROYO SECO PARKWAY, CALIFORNIA, 1940.
California Department of Transportation, Headquarters Photography Unit.

Chapter 3

WHAT YOU NEED TO KNOW

Recognizing you have a historic road requires little more than sensitivity and awareness; knowing what to do to ensure its preservation, however, can be daunting. Where do you begin? This chapter will introduce you to the three issues threatening historic roads (safety, liability, and ignorance) and the four threats to the integrity of historic roads (realignment, destruction, replacement, and regional threats), and present you with an introduction to the basic concepts, theories, and policies useful for the historic roads advocate.

The Three Issues Threatening Historic Roads

To their credit, many of our nation's historic roads still function admirably. Historic roads provide direct and efficient commuting links, take us to places of natural beauty and recreation, and link historic communities. The fact that the general public still uses these resources on a daily basis in many ways diminishes recognition of their historic value.

Today, many historic roads are threatened with changes that will compromise their integrity. What are the driving forces behind these threats? Essentially they are three issues: safety, liability, and ignorance. The three issues have been identified to help you understand the forces behind the loss, or threatened loss, of historic roads.

SAFETY

The provision of a safe driving environment for both motorists and other highway users is of paramount importance. New and advanc-

ing technologies continually offer us greater information and strategies for designing ever safer roadways. For historic roads such technologies bring a mixed blessing. While these new technologies can
offer innovative ways of enhancing safety on historic roads, they may
also bring into action new administrative policies that, when implemented in unsympathetic or generic fashion, may destroy the character of a historic road.

A ONE-LANE TUNNEL ON A LOW-VOLUME ROAD IN WESTERN MARYLAND.
WHAT ARE THE SAFETY IMPLICATIONS? WHAT ARE THE PRESERVATION ISSUES?
Paul Daniel Marriott.

How Safe Is Safe?

*Decisions to change a historic road through reconstruction almost always originate from
a concern, real or perceived, for safety. As you read this book you will be encouraged to
differentiate between real and perceived safety issues. You are asked to challenge decisions that have been made to reconstruct historic roads simply because they do not meet
currently held guidelines for design—not from any demonstrated accident problem. In
general, you are asked to look for creative ways to accommodate safety-inspired changes
on roadways or segments where there are demonstrated accident problems. The question
remains however: how safe is safe?*

*Yellowstone National Park reconstructed roughly one third of the park's roads in the
mid 1990s. The narrow, twisting roads were viewed, with the support of some accident
data, as being unsafe. Therefore, the park roads were widened and straightened in accordance with the recommended guidelines promoted by AASHTO.*

The result of these changes, designed for safety, has been an increase in both the accident rate and wildlife kill. It seems that visitors are driving at a much higher rate of speed now due to the "improved" road. Should the park further widen and straighten these roads to accommodate these new accident statistics? Where does it all end?

Look carefully at safety solutions. The potential exists to lessen overall safety in attempts to improve a single issue.

Safety is a difficult issue to address, and those proposing negative changes to historic roads are likely to cite safety as the primary rationale—legitimating change even if no conclusive records suggest a safety problem. Nevertheless safety is critical, and you must recognize that fact. Your advantage lies in the fact that there is generally more than one way to address safety concerns. You should not accept claims of widespread carnage and destruction if safety changes aren't made without undertaking careful study and review of existing conditions, impacts, and alternative strategies. Transportation agencies maintain records of traffic safety that you should examine to be certain a safety issue really exists. Remember too that some changes designed to enhance safety, in instances, decrease it—removing curves, for example, may actually increase the speed of the average motorist, now able to travel faster on the straighter roadway. Argue safety with safety. *If you or your organization is perceived to be putting preservation ahead of human life, you have little hope of success.*

THE FEAR OF TORT LIABILITY GUIDES MANY OF THE DECISIONS REGARDING THE MANAGEMENT OF HISTORIC ROADS.
Paul Daniel Marriott.

LIABILITY

The United States has become a litigious society. The response to potential liability issues has influenced many areas of our built environment. Historic roads have not been exempt from the latest movement to eliminate any situation that might pose a tort liability risk. Roads gently aligned in the landscape at the beginning of the twentieth century are now being straightened for fear that a driver traveling at an excessive rate of speed will lose control of his or her vehicle and sue the local or state government because the road does not meet currently held design practices. Historic bridges are being destroyed in cases where the lane width is narrower than currently held design practices, even in instances without demonstrated safety problems. In many cases the motivation for such actions has not arisen from excessive accident rates, but rather the fear that such roads, designed to the standards of an earlier time, pose liability issues.

IGNORANCE

In most instances, the destruction or alteration of historic roads for safety or liability has not been due to reckless disregard for the resource, but instead to simple ignorance regarding the historic value of

REPRESENTATIVES FROM THE STATE DOT'S PLANNERS, AND PRESERVATIONISTS DISCUSS ISSUES SURROUNDING CONNECTICUT'S MERRITT PARKWAY AT THE FIRST CONFERENCE ON HISTORIC ROADS (SPONSORED BY NTFHR, THE NATIONAL TRUST FOR HISTORIC PRESERVATION, AND THE WESTCHESTER COUNTY (NEW YORK) DEPARTMENT OF PLANNING, 1995).
Paul Daniel Marriott.

the route. It's not like highway designers are saying "that's a nice historic road—let's do a project to make it ugly or, better yet, to destroy it." The majority of people making the decisions that affect all roads, including historic roads, are trained in the safe and efficient movement of the motoring public. They work with hard facts and figures. Their offices and charges have not traditionally been involved in the identification and management of historic resources. They need to be educated as to the value of these historic resources.

Ticket Please ——————————————————

There are no velvet ropes separating New York's Bronx River Parkway (constructed 1907–1924) from the surrounding community. No admission fees. No guides in period costume to whisk you away on an interpretative tour in a Model T. Perhaps unfortunately, the Bronx River Parkway still functions quite effectively in moving today's modern automobiles. Most of the parkway's daily users are unaware of the road's immense and innovative contributions to transportation design and technology. So, like many urban roads, the Bronx River Parkway constantly faces citizens who clamor for more lanes and faster speeds—unaware that such requests are equivalent to converting the dining room at Thomas Jefferson's Monticello to a food court.

∾ The Four Threats to the Integrity of Historic Roads

Responses to the issues of safety, liability, and ignorance oftentimes threaten the integrity of historic roads. Threats can generally be organized into four key areas: realignment, destruction, replacement, and regional threats.

REALIGNMENT

Realignment refers to the adjustment or movement of the path of the current road. Realignment means that the beginning and ending points of the proposed work tie back into the existing road—in other words, a segment of roadway is to be rebuilt in a different location. Realignment may be as simple as a shift in the lanes to soften a sharp curve or as destructive as several miles of new road abandoning the original alignment. Often realignment is a response to real safety problems—the straightening of a curving stretch of road associated

NEW ALIGNMENT—CREIGHTON BOULEVARD (ORIGINALLY CONSTRUCTED C. 1912),
PART OF THE OMAHA PARKWAY SYSTEM, WAS REALIGNED TO REMOVE THE CURVES
IN THE ORIGINAL DESIGN INSPIRED BY NOTED LANDSCAPE ARCHITECT
H. W. S. CLEVELAND.
Paul Daniel Marriott.

THE ORIGINAL ALIGNMENT OF CREIGHTON BOULEVARD IS STILL DISCERNABLE IN
THE ADAMS PARK LANDSCAPE. CLEVELAND'S PLAN CALLED FOR THE CONSTRUCTION
OF "BROAD ORNAMENTAL AVENUES, KNOWN AS BOULEVARDS OR PARKWAYS."
—H. W. S. CLEVELAND'S REPORT TO THE OMAHA COMMISSIONERS, JUNE 1889.
Paul Daniel Marriott.

with a high accident rate, for example. But sometimes realignment is a reaction to perceived safety problems—the same straightening based on an undocumented belief that such curves are unsafe. Occasionally realignment can be due to other factors such as a change in vehicle use, speed, or volume necessitating a wider or more level road.

DESTRUCTION

Destruction refers to the complete removal of a historic roadway or roadside element. There are two key types of destruction that you may encounter—complete and incremental. The loss of an entire historic road at one time would be *complete destruction*. It is possible that the same destruction could occur over a period of years or even decades through systematic changes, destroying or modifying portions of the original road—for example, the widening of travel lanes, addition of shoulders, or removal of trees—to a point at which the entire road is lost. Such *incremental destruction* can be the result of a concerted policy to rebuild the historic road, or it can occur simply through responses to seemingly unrelated events and policies that, taken in total, lead to the loss of the historic resource.

A HISTORIC STONE BRIDGE AT NATIONAL AIRPORT, WASHINGTON, D.C., BEING DEMOLISHED (1994) FOR AIRPORT EXPANSION.
Paul Daniel Marriott.

Incremental destruction is one of the most pervasive, most devastating, and least monitored activities ruining our historic roads. A bit of historic stone wall here, a small realignment there; a historic light fixture replaced with a galvanized steel alternative; an extra turn lane at a busy intersection. These seemingly small changes—surely changes that no reasonable preservationist would argue with—gradually alter the character of the roadway and build subtle, yet steady movement away from historic character. Before you know it, another historic road is gone. As always, be reasonable, but scrutinize each minor change to determine both the rationale and the cumulative effect.

Destruction may be as simple as the removal of a brick curb, a foot path, the roadside landscape, or an overlook area, or as complete as the rebuilding of several miles of historic road. Remember that incremental destructions, in aggregate, add up to complete destruction.

Replacement

The replacement of road and roadside features deserves careful attention. A historic road is actually a collection of unique details—cobbled gutters, brick pavement, stone bridges, art deco lighting, signs, wooded areas, stone outcroppings, and exquisite concrete balusters. These are all details that, taken in total, provide the richness of the experience. Occasionally, time, wear, or even accidents may necessitate the replacement of an element or elements of a historic road. Every effort should be made to replace roadway and roadside elements with like materials, constructions, and forms in their original locations. The replacement of any historic road feature with one of inferior aesthetic quality, material, or finish chips away at the historic integrity of the route (incremental destruction).

When looking at replacement issues, also remember the issues of authenticity. If, for example, you have a historic boulevard designed in the 1890s that never had streetlights and night lighting has become a safety need, don't allow yourself to be wooed by the promise of charming Victorian lighting, even if it is of the proper period. Such lighting would not be authentic. You must investigate another method to provide the illumination if it is deemed necessary. Similarly, pressed concrete paving bricks, stamped concrete patterns, and interlocking "Z" bricks are not a suitable substitute for historic clay paving bricks.

A RECONSTRUCTED BRIDGE ON THE BRONX RIVER PARKWAY MAKES VAGUE REFERENCE TO THE PARKWAY'S HISTORIC STONE ARCH BRIDGES. THE STEEL DECK BRIDGE WITH STONE-VENEERED ABUTMENTS IS A POOR MATCH FOR REMAINING BRIDGES SUCH AS THE NEARBY ARDSLEY ROAD BRIDGE.
Paul Daniel Marriott.

THE ARDSLEY ROAD BRIDGE, BRONX RIVER PARKWAY.
Paul Daniel Marriott.

THE "4-LEVEL" IN LOS ANGELES, CONSTRUCTED IN 1949, WAS THE FIRST FREEWAY-
TO-FREEWAY INTERCHANGE IN THE NATION. A RECENT PROJECT TO IMPROVE
THE SAFETY OF THE FACILITY REPLACED THE ORIGINAL STREAMLINED
STEEL RAILS (VISIBLE ON THE UPPER TWO LEVELS) WITH A MORE ORNATE
"HISTORIC–STYLE" BARRIER WALL.
Gary Iverson, Caltrans.

Lighting Denver Parkways

The Denver Parkway System, listed in the National Register of Historic Places, was designed in the latter part of the nineteenth century to provide substantial green linkages across the growing city. For some parts of the system not originally illuminated, time, use, and safety eventually demanded lighting for night use.

To meet this new need and to maintain the historic character of the parkways, the city installed tall, simple, dark green fixtures of contemporary design. The new lights "disappear" between the trees, and the lantern (light source), located above the lower tree branches, is practically invisible to the daytime traveler. In areas originally illuminated, these contemporary fixtures have been added as well—their simple design not competing with the ornate historic lighting. The parkways are now well illuminated at night. When you think about it, the introduction of ornate Victorian-style lighting, frequently employed to signify "historic" areas, would have compromised the naturalistic design of the parkways.

THIS SIMPLE, NONOBTRUSIVE LIGHT HAS IMPROVED LIGHTING ON DENVER'S
6TH AVENUE PARKWAY WITH A MINIMUM IMPACT ON THE PARKWAY'S INTEGRITY.
Paul Daniel Marriott.

REGIONAL THREATS

Regional threats and issues address the broader landscape and community associated with the historic road. What is the nature of the
landscape through which the road passes? Is it wooded? Urban? Suburban? Does the historic road wind along a river gorge or pass
through the Great Plains? Are nearby billboards impacting the visual

SUBURBAN SPRAWL CAN INCREASE TRAFFIC VOLUME ON HISTORIC ROADS, TURN
QUAINT CULTURAL ROUTES INTO COMMUTER ROUTES, AND HAVE NEW RESIDENTS
CLAMORING FOR HIGHER SPEEDS AND ADDITIONAL LANES.
Paul Daniel Marriott.

SUBURBANIZATION HAS FORCED MANY HISTORIC ROADS TO ACCOMMODATE
TRAFFIC USES FOR WHICH THEY WERE NOT ORIGINALLY DESIGNED. ROCK CREEK
AND POTOMAC PARKWAY IN WASHINGTON, D.C. FUNCTIONS AS A ONE-WAY
COMMUTER ARTERIAL DURING PEAK HOURS.
Paul Daniel Marriott.

ENTRY SIGN ON ROCK CREEK AND POTOMAC PARKWAY. ON COLUMBUS DAY 1996
A HEAD–ON COLLISION OCCURRED ON THE PARKWAY WHEN A DRIVER ACCUSTOMED
TO ONE–WAY TRAFFIC, FORGOT THE TWO–WAY POLICY ON FEDERAL HOLIDAYS AND
CROSSED THE CENTERLINE OF THE ROAD TO PASS ANOTHER AUTOMOBILE.
Paul Daniel Marriott.

integrity of the route? Is a new highway planned to cross or pass over
or under your historic road?

Regional threats may originate well beyond the actual historic
road itself. Has a sudden increase in population generated increased
traffic on the historic road? Does the historic road provide direct and
easy access to a new employment area, thus generating commuter
traffic? Is a new facility adjacent to the historic road going to visually
impact the historic road or generate an increase in traffic? Are historic views or vistas threatened by any changes?

∾ *Context / Integrity*

Context refers to the historic setting or landscape that represents a
specific period or periods in the road's history. Integrity refers to the
quality of that remaining context.

As with all historic resources, it is impossible to separate a historic
road from its context, its setting. Consider, for example, a parkway

CONTEXT AND INTEGRITY ARE HIGH ALONG ROUTE 66 IN MCLEAN, TEXAS,
AT THIS RESTORED PHILLIPS 66 SERVICE STATION FROM THE 1920S.
National Historic Route 66 Federation.

designed to meander through a river valley or a nineteenth-century
boulevard framed by stately brownstones. If the parkway maintains its
original alignment, but the designed landscape is lost or the river has
been piped underground, is the road still a historic resource, or is it a
fragment of the larger original system? If the boulevard with its
spreading oaks down the median remains intact but the brownstones
have been replaced with fast-food restaurants, discount retailers, and
parking lots, is the boulevard still a historic road? In other words, is
remaining pavement sufficient to claim historic status?

You must evaluate the context of a historic road before you can
make recommendations for its preservation. If the context is in place
but sufficiently degraded, you may not be looking at preservation,
but rehabilitation. In such instances, interpretation of the historic
corridor may be more appropriate than preservation.

In a similar manner, you must evaluate the integrity of the route.
Consider the aforementioned parkway with the river channelized for
flood control. The context is in place (the river is still flowing), but
the integrity has been diminished. In like manner, imagine the

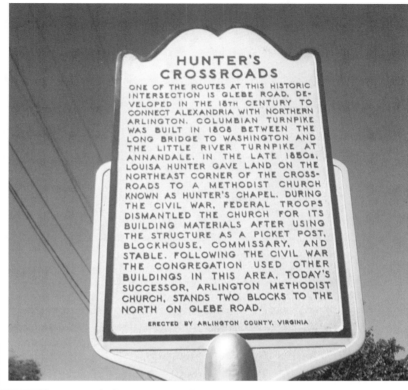

HUNTER'S CROSSROADS IN ARLINGTON, VIRGINIA, HAS BEEN AN
IMPORTANT INTERSECTION SINCE THE EARLY NINETEENTH CENTURY.
LIKE MANY HISTORIC ROADS, HOWEVER, SIGNIFICANT GROWTH AND
CHANGE HAVE OBLITERATED THE INTERSECTION'S HISTORIC CONTEXT.
Paul Daniel Marriott.

HISTORIC GLEBE ROAD APPROACHING HUNTER'S CROSSROADS.
Paul Daniel Marriott.

GUARDRAIL, JERSEY BARRIERS, AND MESH LIGHT SCREEN ADDITIONS HAVE
OBSCURED THIS STONE AND CONCRETE VIADUCT ON THE BRONX RIVER PARKWAY.
WHILE THE STRUCTURE DOES EXIST BENEATH THESE MODERN SAFETY-INSPIRED
ADDITIONS, ITS INTEGRITY HAS BEEN LOST.
Paul Daniel Marriott.

MAINTAINING A HIGH LEVEL OF INTEGRITY CAN BE DIFFICULT, ESPECIALLY FOR
ROADS WITH MULTIPLE LAYERS OF HISTORY. DUE TO SPECIAL CONSIDERATIONS
(NOT TO MENTION TOURISM REVENUES), WILLIAMSBURG, VIRGINIA, MAINTAINS AN
18TH-CENTURY INTEGRITY BY CLOSING THE HISTORIC DUKE OF GLOUCESTER
STREET DAILY.
Paul M. Marriott, Jr. / Colonial Parents Photography.

boulevard brownstones clad in vinyl siding with aluminum replacement windows. How have these changes impacted the integrity of the historic road? Do such changes invalidate any claims of historic significance, or do they simply offer additional challenges to the historic road preservationist?

Quite obviously, context and integrity are difficult judgments to make for many historic roads. They are important concepts to address at the start of any historic road advocacy project. You must have a clear idea of what you are trying to preserve.

Historic Bell or Taco Bell

Few travelers along a busy commercial strip in San Bruno, just south of San Francisco, notice the California historical marker and antique bell acknowledging El Camino Real. The bell, located alongside a motel parking lot, marks the route of the colonial "Royal Way"—El Camino Real—in Spanish California. El Camino Real linked the mission settlements up and down the Pacific coast and was the principal overland trade route. As a well-located and well-connected artery, El Camino Real, like many historic roads, grew and developed with the rest of California. Today this corridor of bright lights, discount shopping, and drive-thrus little resembles the dusty corridor of 200 years ago. Is El Camino Real a historic road, or is El Camino Real a historic corridor?

EL CAMINO REAL TODAY SOUTH OF SAN FRANCISCO. IS THIS A HISTORIC ROAD?
Paul Daniel Marriott.

HISTORIC MARKERS, SUCH AS THIS ONE IN SAN BRUNO, MARK THE ROUTE OF
EL CAMINO REAL ALONG THE CALIFORNIA COAST.
Paul Daniel Marriott.

Law and Policy

The laws and policies described in this section can provide significant
protection for historic resources. You cannot, however, expect them
to be benevolently bestowed on your historic road by thoughtful
agencies and officials. These laws and policies are provided as part of a
system of checks and balances aiding in the cause of preservation.
Their effective application often depends on concerned and vigilant
citizens who invoke their use to advance historic preservation.

National Register
of Historic Places

The National Register of Historic Places is maintained by the National Park Service. Listing in the National Register is the principal form of recognition for historic properties in the United States. Historic roads, bridges, buildings, and structures and the landscapes associated with historic roads are all potentially eligible for listing in the National Register. There are approximately 60 historic roads listed in the National Register and included here in **Appendix A.** (This number is based on listings for which the road is a principal part of the nomination. There are numerous additional references for which a road is a minor reference—these have not been included in this listing.)

You can request that a road be listed in the National Register by preparing a nomination form and submitting it to your State Historic Preservation officer. These forms reviewed by the National Park Service, provide an in-depth history of the resource in question and documentation of current conditions. If the property in question meets National Register criteria, it will be listed.

While a listing in the National Register may provide valuable recognition of the resource, *it does not provide any guarantees or protections* for the listed property unless some federal approval, permitting, or funding is involved in an action that would threaten or adversely affect the resource. In such cases the preservation laws described in this chapter may be triggered. Even then, if it can be demonstrated that there is a *compelling* reason why such federal action provides greater benefit to the public, or if it can be shown that there is no *viable* alternative, a listed property can be significantly altered or destroyed. A private owner may alter or even destroy a National Register listed property whenever he or she desires, provided, of course, that such action does not require a permit from a federal agency or violate any state or local laws.

National Register Criteria
for Evaluation

The National Register of Historic Places has established the following criteria to evaluate the worthiness of properties for listing in the National Register:

The quality of significance in American history, architecture, archaeology, engineering, and culture is present in districts, sites, buildings, structures, and objects that possess integrity of location, design, setting, materials, workmanship, feeling, and association and

A. that are associated with the events that have made a significant contribution to the broad patterns of our history; or
B. that are associated with the lives of persons significant in our past; or
C. that embody the distinctive characteristics of a type, period, or method of construction, or that represent the work of a master, or that possess high artistic values, or that represent a significant and distinguishable entity whose components may lack individual distinction; or
D. that have yielded, or may be likely to yield, information important in prehistory or history.

Determination of Eligibility for Listing in the National Register

Listing in the National Register is an involved process requiring a commitment to research and documentation to support the case of the historic property in question. For projects with a federal involvement, a Determination of Eligibility (DOE) for listing in the National Register documents significant historic properties without undertaking the rigorous listing process. A DOE is made by the State Historic Preservation Officer based on evidence of the property's qualities. The Pulaski Skyway in New Jersey and the Arroyo Seco Parkway in California have been determined eligible for listing in the National Register.

A DOE does not provide all of the benefits of listing, such as tax benefits, but it does trigger the protection of Section 106 and 4(f), which will be discussed in the next section.

Preservation Laws

In addition to the obvious benefits and protections these preservation laws provide, such laws may provide you with standing to sue if it can be demonstrated that the required reviews have not been fair or thorough.

The National Historic Preservation Act (NHPA) of 1966

Section 101

The National Historic Preservation Act of 1966 mandates that each state have a State Historic Preservation Officer or SHPO (popularly called a "Ship-o" or "Shhh-po"depending on where you live) to oversee the federal policies outlined in the NHPA, 16 U.S.C. §470a. The SHPO is appointed by the governor and makes recommendations regarding listing and the DOE for listing in the National Register. See **Appendix C** for a listing of state historic preservation offices.

Section 106

Popularly referred to as just Section 106, Section 106 of the NHPA, 16 U.S.C. § 470f, requires all federal agencies to "take into account" the effects of their actions on historic sites. Section 106 applies only to historic sites that are eligible for or listed in the National Register of Historic Places. These actions include federally sponsored or funded projects as well as private activities and projects that are subject to federal licensing, permitting, or approval. If the proposed action will have an "effect" on a historic property, the agency must consult with the SHPO and possibly the Advisory Council on Historic Preservation, an independent federal agency, prior to approving or funding the project. The purpose of consultation is to seek ways to avoid or mitigate any adverse effect. The consultation usually results in a binding memorandum of agreement (MOA) among the involved agency (a State DOT, for example), the SHPO, and sometimes the Advisory Council. An MOA may, for example, require the involvement of consulting parties—such as a historic preservation group—in the process, or it might identify a specific course of action—archaeological digs, for example. The Advisory Council does not have the authority to stop a project, although an objection from the Council may carry considerable political weight.

Section 110

Section 110 of the NHPA mandates that all federal agencies must have a management plan for historic resources owned or controlled by the agency (16 U.S.C. § 470h-2). Section 110 states that "all Federal agencies shall assume responsibility for the preservation of historic properties which are owned or controlled by such agency." The law states specifically, "Each Federal agency shall establish... a preservation program for the identification, evaluation, and documentation to the National Register of Historic Places, and protection of historic properties." The law further notes that such properties are to be "managed and maintained in a way that considers the preservation of their historic, archaeological, architectural, and cultural values in compliance with section 106." (NHPA, Sec. 110)

All federal agency actions that may potentially impact historic resources (regardless of ownership) are subject to Section 106. Section 110 mandates the overall substantive management responsibilities for federally owned or controlled properties. Additionally, Section 110 specifically warns against actions that are undertaken to deliberately degrade the quality of a historic resource (such as anticipatory demolition or negligent maintenance practices) to avoid Section 106 review.

The Department of Transportation Act of 1966

Section 4(f)

Section 4(f) of the Department of Transportation Act of 1966, 49 U.S.C. § 303, is a substantive requirement that prohibits federal approval or funding of any transportation project that requires the "use" of any historic site, public park, recreation area, or wildlife refuge unless there is "no feasible and prudent alternative to the project" and "all possible planning to minimize harm to the project" has been addressed. (DOT Act, 1966, Sec. 4[f]) In addition to the direct physical taking of land, the term *use* also includes any indirect effects that would "substantially impair" the value of the protected sites. For example, *use* could include the effect of noise, vibrations, and visual intrusion from a new freeway on an adjacent historic house. The 4(f) determination may be a separate document or part of an EIS (defined later) and is subject to public comment.

You should note that many transportation projects, even at the local level, receive federal funding and involve the Federal Highway Administration (FHWA). It is quite possible, for example, that a minor bridge rehabilitation in your community has federal money involved and would require 4(f) review. Unlike Section 106, which applies only to sites that are listed in, or eligible for (DOE), the National Register, 4(f) applies to a much broader range of sites, such as public parks and wildlife refuges. Remember too, 4(f) applies only to the U.S. Department of Transportation, whereas Section 106 applies to all federal agencies.

National Environmental Policy Act of 1969

Commonly referred to as NEPA (nee-pa), the National Environmental Policy Act of 1969, 42 U.S.C. § 4332(2)(C), is a procedural requirement for federal agencies to disclose and consider the impacts of all "major federal actions significantly affecting the quality of the human environment." To meet this requirement, an agency must prepare an Environmental Impact Statement (EIS), an Environmental Assessment (EA), or a Categorical Exclusion (CE). These documents, while generally recognized for their assessment of impacts on environmental features such as wetlands or endangered wildlife, are also required to include an assessment of impacts on "urban quality, historic and cultural resources, and the design of the built environment." NEPA is applicable to all federally sponsored, funded, or licensed projects.

An EA is prepared for actions that do not typically require an EIS. On completion of the EA, if there has been a "Finding of No Significant Impact" (FONSI), the project can proceed. An EA may also make the determination that a full EIS is needed for more intensive review and analysis. Both documents (EIS and EA), must be circulated to interested agencies and to the general public for comment.

Remember, more than one of these statutes can be triggered by a project. For example, even if an EIS does determine resources to be of significance, if the DOT or other agency can demonstrate that there is no prudent or feasible alternative to the proposed construction, the project can continue. At the same time, many transportation projects that result in FONSI determinations will nonetheless go through compliance with Section 106 and 4(f).

Be Wary of the Experts

There is a fine line between distrust and caution. Do be cautious, however, of experts hired to make independent determinations as to the significance of the historic resource or its suitability or practicality for preservation. Such consultants are frequently hired to develop the impact statements that are used in Section 106, 4(f), and NEPA reviews and may or may not have had much experience in historic preservation. Such reports can choose to promote the positive or the negative aspects of preservation. Investigate the experience of the firm. Study other reports they have prepared and talk to the preservation organizations in communities in which they have previously worked. Firms with little experience in historic structures, for example, may underestimate the feasibility of preservation. Try to approach the road management entity before the consultant is selected and offer your assistance in selecting a consultant.

Similarly, if your organization is conducting any studies, be sure that your consultants are well skilled in transportation issues as well as historic preservation issues. Inconclusive or inaccurate findings by an organization representing your group can jeopardize your credibility. Remember, every issue will have several different approaches or points of view.

THE SURFACE TRANSPORTATION AND UNIFORM RELOCATION ASSISTANCE ACT (STURAA) OF 1987

STURAA, 23 U.S.C. § 144(o), contains two special provisions for protecting historic bridges. First, prior to the approval of federal funding for the demolition of any historic bridge, STURRA requires the bridge be made available to a "state, local, or responsible private entity" that would agree to maintain the bridge. Second, STURAA obligates the FHWA to reimburse or make available to the new owner the costs of preserving or rehabilitating a historic bridge that is no longer used for motor vehicle traffic, up to the estimated cost of bridge demolition. At this time, the use of STURAA makes a bridge ineligible for any future federal transportation funding. Funding for regular maintenance and repair must be secured from another source. (At the time of publication there was an initiative to enable STURAA bridges to receive federal funding for routine maintenance. Please consult with your state DOT regarding particulars.)

STATE AND LOCAL PRESERVATION LAWS

Most states and many local governments have laws governing historic resources. Their applicability to historic roads varies significantly by state and jurisdiction. In general, however, many states have laws similar to NEPA, Section 106, and occasionally Section 4(f) in that they apply to state-funded projects. They offer a second tier of protection for historic resources that may not be threatened by projects funded with federal dollars. Approximately 1,800 municipalities in the United States have enacted historic preservation ordinances.[1] A listing of state historic preservation offices nationwide is included in **Appendix C**. Contact these offices for details regarding your particular state.

TORT LIABILITY

When dealing with historic roads you are likely to come across the term *tort liability*. The fear of tort liability is frequently cited by road management entities when proposing destructive changes to historic roads.

A tort is a wrong—a private or civil injury, for example. Liability refers to a legal obligation or responsibility. Tort liability addresses situations in which an injury or harm has occurred due to a breach of a preexisting duty or obligation that results in potential exposure for damages. For example, consider the situation surrounding a movie patron injured due to smoke inhalation at a theater that failed to provide emergency egress during a fire. First, the theater owner had an *obligation* to provide an emergency exit; second, a *breach* occurred when the theater exit was blocked; third, an *injury* occurred due to that blocked exit.

Tort liability as it relates to a roadway can be interpreted this way: A preexisting legal *obligation* exists for the state or local government or other road management agency to maintain the road in a safe manner. Naturally this obligation varies from state to state and from road type to road type. If the responsible agency has failed in its duty to maintain the roadway in a safe manner, a *breach* of that duty has occurred. If someone is *injured* due to that breach of responsibility, that individual may take the responsible agency to court to sue for damages. Again, tort liability exists only if the managing agency failed to comply with the legal standard of care for maintaining and operating the road. If an injury is caused by some other factor, tort liability may not exist.

Tort liability varies from state to state. In some states local governments have limited or full *sovereign immunity* (meaning that the state or local government cannot be held liable for government actions). In some states public agencies may have full sovereign immunity, but their officials may not.

Limiting Liability on Kansas Bridges

Informal Opinion of the Kansas Attorney General Regarding the Liability of Local Governments for Historic Bridges

Carla J. Stovall, the Attorney General of Kansas, issued an informal opinion regarding the potential tort liability of local governmental entities with respect to the repair and maintenance of historic bridges in 1995.[2] The informal opinion was requested by the Kansas Historical Society to assist local communities in preserving historic bridges facing threats from design standards. An informal opinion is not promulgated as official state policy. Its purpose is to provide credible and sound reasoning regarding a particular circumstance—in this case, historic bridges. The Kansas Attorney General's analysis is extremely helpful to preservation advocates who are confronted with arguments about liability from state and local governments. Remember, the courts will often cite related cases or laws from other states to justify a decision. Even though such references as well as references to informal opinions are not binding, they nevertheless become a part of a body of knowledge justifying a particular decision. Please note that not all state attorney general offices issue informal opinions.

In the informal opinion, Attorney General Stovall notes that the Kansas Tort Claims Act frees local government entities from liability and damages resulting from bridge design if the plans were "prepared in conformity with the generally recognized and prevailing standards in existence at the time such plan or design was prepared...." In other words, the informal opinion suggests that historic bridges that are maintained in good condition, free of demonstrated or chronic safety problems, and built to acceptable standards of their day should not be a liability burden for local communities. Consider a Kansas bridge a few feet narrower than recommended by current design guidelines. Under this informal opinion, the Kansas Attorney General suggests that bridge width itself is not a liability issue. Should an accident occur, the injured party cannot rely on bridge width alone as evidence of the local government not fulfilling its obligation to provide a safe roadway. Another breach in the government's responsibility must be demonstrated.

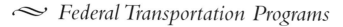
∿ *Federal Transportation Programs*

THE INTERMODAL SURFACE TRANSPORTATION EFFICIENCY ACT (ISTEA) OF 1991

ISTEA (generally referred to as "ice-tea") has reinvented transportation policy in the United States. It has radically altered the way in which transportation policy and decisions are made at the federal, state, and local levels. ISTEA encourages alternative and coordinated means of transportation, advocates greater citizen input and comment regarding transportation decisions, streamlines federal involvement at the state and local levels, and encourages an improvement of the quality of the transportation users' experience.

The idea of recognizing the quality of the transportation experience is the component of ISTEA generating the greatest interest in the preservation community. The quality of transportation experiences and the programs by which such experiences may be improved are referred to under ISTEA as *enhancements.* Enhancements form a broad category addressing everything from bike trails and public art to environmental restoration and land easements. Each state is allowed relative freedom in establishing enhancement programs, and, as a result, enhancements have been interpreted very broadly by some states and very narrowly by others.

For the historic roads advocate, ISTEA is clear and direct regarding the use of enhancement funds for historic roads. Section 1007c of ISTEA, amending 23 U.S.C. §101(a), defines federal funding for transportation enhancements as follows:

> The term transportation enhancement activities' means, with respect to any project or the area to be served by the project, provision of facilities for pedestrians and bicycles, acquisition of scenic easements and scenic or historic sites, scenic or **historic highway programs, landscaping and other scenic beautification, historic preservation, rehabilitation and operation of historic transportation buildings, structures, or facilities...** control and removal of outdoor advertising, archaeological planning and research, and mitigation of water pollution due to highway runoff. (emphasis added) (ISTEA, Sec. 1007c)

Funding categories under ISTEA include interstate maintenance, bridge, National Highway System, surface transportation programs, and others. For every state, 10% of all designated federal transportation funds under the Surface Transportation Programs must be used for enhancements. There are 11 eligible categories for funding under Surface Transportation Programs (Section 133, Title 23, U.S.C.): construction/reconstruction/rehabilitation, capital improvements for transportation, carpool/bike projects, highway and transit safety, highway and transit research and development, traffic control, planning, transportation enhancements, air quality, management, and environmental mitigation. This funding covers everything from new city busses and commuter rail to freeway construction and wetlands cleanup. The 10% for enhancements is a general fund to be used for all enhancements statewide. A state is not required to obligate the enhancement funds by transportation type. For example, a state that allocates 20% of transportation funds to commuter rail need not allocate 20% of enhancement funds to commuter rail. Further, it should be noted that states are not limited to 10% funding for enhancements—this is a minimum. As one of the 11 eligible categories for the Surface Transportation Programs, a state may elect to spend any amount above the 10% minimum for transportation enhancements. Historic roads advocates should further note that one category of the Surface Transportation Programs provides funding for research and development. Researching safety on historic roads, for example, is an eligible project for funding.

1997 is the last year for current ISTEA funding. At this time there are efforts under way to continue enhancement funding under the next federal transportation program. Please consult with your state regarding the status of enhancement funds. NEXTEA, National Economic Crossroads Transportation Efficiency Act will continue ISTEA.

National Highway System (NHS)

The National Highway System (NHS) refers to a newly designated category of roads intended to represent the primary highway network for the United States. The NHS designated a series of interstate and primary routes (arterials) as our official primary transportation network for the automobile. Unlike the interstate building program of the 1950s, 1960s, and 1970s, the NHS has been established primarily on existing roads—it was not envisioned as a road-building project. The NHS includes roughly 165,000 of the nation's approximately 4 million miles of roadway. All NHS roads are required to meet Federal Highway Administration guidelines and policies for safety, design, and maintenance.

The benefit of the NHS to state and local governments and the preservation community is the new flexibility available to non-NHS roads. Past requirements accompanying federal funds have been relaxed for non-NHS roads, allowing state and local governments greater latitude and discretion in how a project is approached. States now have a greater incentive to develop statewide highway design standards under this new policy. Such standards have the potential, with the support and encouragement of the preservation community, to greatly benefit historic roads through special designs, policies, and flexibilities tailored to their distinctive needs.

Please note that, while the NHS will allow greater flexibility in local and state decision making, Section 106 will still apply regardless of a road's NHS status.

PLANNING

ISTEA has provisions for metropolitan and statewide planning to facilitate greater interaction of transportation decisions in comprehensive planning. Metropolitan planning organizations (MPOs) are responsible for developing, in cooperation with the state government and appropriate transportation agencies, a long-range transportation plan addressing the region's needs and a transportation improvement plan (TIP) addressing strategies to enhance the transportation experience. The MPO must address—in addition to traditional transportation activities—land use, intermodal connectivity (a bike path linking to a light-rail line, for example), and methods to enhance transit service.

The statewide planning provision under ISTEA mandates a statewide planning process, a statewide transportation plan, and a statewide transportation program. The statewide TIP must be consistent with the long-range plan.

~ RRR Projects

The three Rs—resurfacing, restoration, and rehabilitation (RRR)—refer to federally funded projects addressing pavement condition and minor modifications to the design of existing roads. RRR projects are not routine maintenance projects. Typically they include resurfacing, the addition of shoulders, the widening of lanes or shoulders, and safety improvements such as the addition of guardrail or warning signs. RRR projects may also include minor realignments, bridge modification, and the removal of roadside hazards. RRR projects have the responsibility of improving the safety of the existing road in a manner as practicable and financially feasible as possible.

For historic roads, RRR projects are frequently encountered. In general, the recommended guidelines for roads undergoing RRR projects are less stringent than those recommended for new construction in the AASHTO Green Book (discussed in the next chapter). However, you should be aware that many states still apply Green Book recommendations for new construction to RRR projects. Furthermore, the application of such policies is at the discretion of the state, making any comments regarding cause and effect for historic roads highly difficult.

The Transportation Research Board (TRB) has made some observations regarding the effectiveness of RRR projects and their impact on a road's safety. TRB notes that "despite more than one-half century of modern road building, knowledge of the safety consequences of highway design decisions is limited."[3] The TRB further notes that "although designers can rely on standards and design aids in many instances, some decisions must be based on site-specific circumstances and judgment." (*Safer Roads,* p. 12) In other words, we still know relatively little about the direct effects of safety improvements to existing roads. Will the addition of a shoulder and wider lanes provide the driver greater maneuverability to avoid an accident, or will such a change lead to increased speed and ultimately a higher accident rate?

Remembering the importance of context, just discussed, and the role of expectancy—how a driver tends to respond to different and predictable environments (discussed in the next chapter)—is essential to the safe management of historic roads. TRB states clearly that the "degree of hazard inherent in a specific feature, such as a narrow bridge, sharp curve, or a roadway without shoulders, depends not only on the feature itself but also on the nature of the nearby roadway environment." (*Safer Roads,* p. 105) Does a newly widened bridge on a narrow park road improve safety? Or are there additional factors that must also be weighed in the decision to widen the bridge—its location, the approach, its accident history?

∾ *Manual on Uniform Traffic Control Devices for Streets and Highways (MUTCD)*

The Manual on Uniform Traffic Control Devices for Streets and Highways depicts national standards for roadway signing, signalization, and channelization as well as standards for marking highways in the United States.[4] The *MUTCD* establishes the "national standard for all traffic control devices installed on any street, highway, or bicycle trail open to public travel." (*MUTCD,* p. vii) It is a publication of the FHWA, developed in cooperation with local, state, and industry representatives with expertise in traffic control. This straightforward, no-nonsense manual addresses issues such as the exact location for a stop sign at an intersection or the appropriate use of a "food, gas, and lodging" sign. As a historic roads advocate, you should be aware of the manual.

Although the *MUTCD* is unlikely to play a major role in advancing the preservation of your historic road in a significant way, it may provide some detailed information that will enhance your overall efforts. The *MUTCD* could become an issue with your historic road if proposed signage, modeled on historic precedent, conflicts with currently held recommendations in the manual. The most recent edition was published in 1988; it is revised as needed.

The *MUTCD* is divided into nine parts: Part I—General Provisions; Part II—Signs; Part III—Markings; Part IV—Signals; Part V—Islands; Part VI—Traffic Controls for Street and Highway Construction, Maintenance, Utility and Emergency Operations; Part VII—Traffic Controls for School Areas; Part VIII—Traffic Control Systems for

ROUTE SHIELDS ALONG THE PALLISADES INTERSTATE PARKWAY, NEW JERSEY AND
NEW YORK.
Paul Daniel Marriott.

Railroad-Highway Grade Crossings; Part IX—Traffic Controls for
Bicycle Facilities.

There are sections in the manual that may be of assistance when
managing a historic road. One of these is Section 2A-6, Excessive
Use of Signs, which states: "Care should be taken not to install too
many signs. A conservative use of regulatory and warning signs is recommended as these signs, if used to excess, tend to lose their effectiveness." (*MUTCD,* p. 2A-3)

On many historic roads, liability concerns have generated an extreme number of warning and regulatory signs. In some instances it
appears that these signs are erected more to demonstrate a commitment to safety by the management entity than to address safety and
driver behavior.

These sections in Part II may also be of assistance: Section 2D-42,
Rest Area Signs; Section 2D-43, Scenic Area Signs; Section 2I-1-7,
Tourist Oriented Directional Signs (TODS).

Copies of MUTCD *are available from:*
  Government Printing Office
  Superintendent of Documents
  710 North Capitol Street, NW
  Washington, DC 20402

Request:
MUTCD, 1988 Edition
Stock No. 050-001-00308-2

∼ Speed

It is essential that the historic roads advocate understand the role of speed in the design and management process. Speed is the single most defining characteristic of how we use a road—65 miles per hour (mph) and higher on our interstates; 20 mph in a school zone. Every aspect of road design changes as speed changes. You can safely brake in approximately 30 feet when traveling at 20 mph—a desirable situation when small children are present. That distance increases to approximately 380 to 650 feet (depending on automobile type and road conditions) when traveling at 65 mph. Speed carries similar extreme roadway differences if you look at the impact of crashing into another automobile at 20 mph versus 65 mph (fender bender versus serious injury) or your ability to read a regulatory sign—as speed increases the letter size on signs must increase to ensure visibility. In other words, think about how many yard sale signs, clearly legible on 10-inch by 12-inch poster board on your neighborhood street, you'd be able to read when cruising by on the interstate at 65 mph?

Speed impacts everything. As the allowable speed of a roadway goes up or down, all aspects of that road's design and management change.

Design Speed versus Posted Speed

Design speed refers to the maximum safe speed for which a road is designed. This is usually higher than the posted speed—the speed limit on the signs along the highway. For example, many interstates are designed to speeds well above 65 mph. The purpose of designing roads to speeds higher than posted is to provide an additional measure of safety should a driver exceed the posted limit. Unfortunately, such design often leads to speeding, as the road is easily and comfortably handled at speeds well above those posted.

∼

Many people are quick to argue that increased enforcement can reduce speed. While this may be true, you should be aware that this argument carries little weight for overall roadway management. An argument for the design of a road based on posted speed, especially if drivers are uniformly traveling at a higher rate of speed, is difficult to support. It comes down to this: If the safe design of the road depends on the enforcement of the posted speed (which may or may not be safe for travelers exceeding that speed) we must, in theory, be able to guarantee that enforcement is available 24 hours a day. Naturally you will have difficulty finding a jurisdiction willing to commit to such enforcement because if enforcement is missing for just 10 minutes—a police coffee break for example—the road manager could be accused of not maintaining the road in a safe manner. No jurisdiction can guarantee enforcement presence at all locations along the historic road all day every day. While police radar can be an effective tool, it is better to work for designs that encourage drivers to slow down.

Traffic Fatalities

As a historic roads advocate you must be aware of the importance of traffic fatalities in the roadway decision-making process. The prevention of the loss of human life on our nation's highways directs many of the decisions regarding roadway design, and the preservation community must understand the need to improve safety to reduce traffic fatalities. In many jurisdictions, a single fatality can do more to alter the way in which a road is managed than dozens of fender benders. As with many situations in the management of all roads, there are instances in which the responses to road design and management as the result of a fatality, while well intentioned, do not necessarily enhance the safety of the road. Such responses may represent the heightened emotional state of the community or it may be a high-profile political response to demonstrate the manager's concern and responsiveness to the incident—for example, cutting down *all* the trees along the road after one has been struck.

Statistics on traffic fatalities for the United States are collected and interpreted by the National Highway Traffic Safety Administration (NHTSA) of the U.S. Department of Transportation. The numbers

ACCIDENTS AND THE FEAR OF TRAFFIC FATALITIES HAVE LONG GUIDED ROAD DESIGN
IN THE UNITED STATES. MANY OF THE ROADS OF THE EARLY TWENTIETH CENTURY
ADVANCED INNOVATIVE, SAFE DESIGNS. THE BRONX RIVER PARKWAY WAS THE
FIRST AUTOMOBILE ROUTE TO USE SEPARATED GRADE INTERCHANGES AND
NIGHTTIME LIGHTING OUTSIDE OF AN URBAN AREA. DESPITE SUCH INNOVATIONS,
ACCIDENTS STILL OCCURRED, SUCH AS THIS ONE IN 1922.
Courtesy of the Westchester (N.Y.) County Archives.

collected represent fatalities on all roads lawfully open to the public
and are complied by each state for NHTSA. The most recent statistics available are from 1995. A few of the numbers are included here
for your reference.[5]

Total traffic fatalities in the United States in 1995
    (includes auto occupants, pedestrians, bicyclists,
    and other road users)   41,798
Total fatal crashes in the United States in 1995
    (this is the number of crashes, a *crash* may involve
    multiple fatalities)   37,221
Pedestrian fatalities (13.4% of the total)   5,585
Bicyclist fatalities (2.0% of the total, 60% of all
    bike fatalities occurred in urban areas)   830

Fatal crashes by speed

12.3%	30 mph or less
17.1%	35–40 mph
16.9%	45–50 mph
44.9%	over 55 mph
6.4%	60 mph or higher

Fatal crashes: collision with a fixed object (a percentage of total fatal crashes) Note: Collisions with fixed objects accounted for only 14.4% of all crashes (over 6 million including fatal injury and property damage), but they accounted for 29.5% of fatal crashes.

1.1%	Bridge
5.1%	Pole or post
2.8%	Guardrail
7.7%	Shrubbery/Tree

Of the 7.7% of the fatal crashes associated with shrubbery or a tree, 51.3% of these involved a driver with a blood alcohol content (BAC) of .01 or higher (note: 41.3% of fatal crashes with tree or shrubbery involve BAC of .1 or higher). When reviewing statistics, remember to consider all the possible influences affecting their origin. The fatality rate involving trees, when those fatalities involving alcohol are removed, suggests that trees and shrubbery alone present a minor traffic safety threat. A drunk driver is far more likely to strike another automobile than a tree. (*Traffic Safety,* p. 54, Table 32) Should we remove all cars from the road when a drunk driver approaches?

∽ *Accident Reporting*

No matter how significant your historic road resource may be, if there is a documented problem with accidents, you cannot overlook the issue of safety. But wait! Before you are too quick to compromise historic preservation due to accident statistics, check the method by which the state or local jurisdiction recorded accidents.

The way in which accidents are reported varies widely from jurisdiction to jurisdiction and state to state. In some areas accidents are reported in precise locations with details noting weather conditions or other influences. In other areas, accidents are simply recorded by road segment; i.e., within predefined areas along the road. This may even be a strip that is several miles long. For example, it may be reported that the accident occurred on Jones Road between mile marker 10 and mile marker 12.

Now, given the scenario of the less accurate reporting method just defined, imagine the ramifications such reporting could have for a historic road. If the 2-mile stretch of Jones Road has a historic bridge (slightly narrower than those constructed today), it may be assumed too quickly that the source of accidents in this segment is the bridge. Is it possible other locational or design factors are actually contributing to the accidents in the segment (off-road distractions such as billboards or higher speeds in straight flat sections)? Of course the answer is yes. Do road managers typically investigate less obvious potential accident causes? Not always.

Big Burger, Big Risk?

For some historic roads, the proliferation of large modern billboards has compromised the historic context and scenic quality of the route. But beyond issues of aesthetics, research shows that billboards can pose a distinct safety risk to the motoring public. The U.S. Fourth Circuit Court of Appeals noted that "no empirical studies are necessary for reasonable people to conclude that billboards pose a traffic hazard, since by their very nature they are designed to distract drivers and their passengers from maintaining a view of the road." [6] Even the Institute of Outdoor Advertising states, "Outdoor's sheer physical size allows for eyestopping, bigger-than-life illustrations." Regarding night billboard impacts, the Institute states, "There is only eyestopping visual display emblazoned across the sky."

Several states, including North Carolina, Ohio, and California, have cited motorist safety as a legitimate rationale for the removal of billboards. A FHWA report in 1980 noted, "There is a positive correlation between the existence of signs and accident rates." [7]

However, for some historic roads, billboards were a key component of the traveler's experience. Before you are too quick to argue a billboard ban, investigate the history of outdoor advertising along your historic road. Burma Shave signs and Mail Pouch Tobacco barns contributed to the character of roads earlier this century. If your road does have a history of outdoor advertising, how did the signs (size, shape, lighting) differ from those of today? Is there a way in which modern advertising can recognize historic precedent?

∼ Inconsistency in the Application of Standards

While many threats to the integrity of historic roads come from changes in use or are generated by safety responses to liability concerns, it can be argued that many of the destructive actions occurring on and along our historic roads have come from the inconsistent, irregular, or inappropriate application of the current recommended guidelines or standards. Because historic roads possess unique qualities and characteristics, they must be viewed differently from all other roadways. For example, the design distinctions (scenic views or street trees) and the multiuse nature (pedestrian trails, interpretative panels) of some historic roads, such as the parkway corridor, represent a unique combination of attributes not typically found within any of the standard highway classification systems.

Frequently, and understandably, many local and state highway departments, lacking the resources to sensitively manage historic roads, apply current standards and expectations to roads designed in the past. Due to the lack of policies and design standards tailored to historic roads, compounded by the heightened awareness for safety and liability issues in recent years, management agencies often apply the toughest standards to avoid the possibility of a citation of contributory negligence in the event of an accident. In many instances, historic roads, due to the lack of clarity as to their position in the transportation world, have been held by the courts to the highest standards. As a result, sections of historic roads that may have the characteristics of a low-volume rural road are, in some cases, being held accountable to arterial or even freeway design standards.

Since all concerned with historic roads have as the ultimate goal the provision of a safe driving environment, it seems reckless to continue depending on limited review and interpretation of the Green Book without investigating the flexibilities that are available. Only with a clear and reasonable expectation of the uses of these roadways can the aesthetic concerns for historic resources be effectively studied and managed.

Green Means Go

State DOTs will always cite the safety of the motoring public in explaining the strict adherence to state design standards. It should be noted however that what appears as a rigid adherence to standards or commitment to policy does have flexibility if need be. Consider Interstate 66 in Fairfax County, Virginia. Hardly a historic road, I-66 is a primary east-west corridor in a rapidly developing area west of Washington, D.C. Due to intensive commuter use, frequent backups, and major constituent complaints, the Virginia Department of Transportation (VDOT) opened the highway's shoulders for use as additional lanes during rush hour periods. In essence, this decision removed the element of a "forgiving roadside environment" promoted by the Green Book for breakdowns and eliminated the deceleration lane prior to exit ramps.

ELECTRONIC LANE INDICATORS ON INTERSTATE 66 IN VIRGINIA.
Paul Daniel Marriott.

Today large electronic green arrows and red Xs signal the availability of the shoulders for use, and signs stating "Begin Exiting Here" encourage through shoulder traffic to yield to exiting traffic. Why was this done? Certainly it has lessened the safety of the route. It is clear the political pressure to move more people during peak periods enabled this departure from standard safe design. Imagine if the same political will to preserve a historic road were felt in the statehouse or the DOT offices.

Details

ART DECO DETAILS FROM THE FULLERTON STREET BRIDGE TO THE LIGHTING AND
SIGN POSTS CREATE A STRONG VOCABULARY FOR LAKE SHORE DRIVE IN CHICAGO
IN THE 1940S.
Courtesy Chicago Park District, Special Collections.

The preservation of authentic roadway details is one of the most important ways to maintain the integrity of a historic road. Much of what we enjoy in life, when you think about it, is the quality of details. The largest project is composed of details. The richness of a local stone, a granite curb versus a concrete one, the flowering shrubbery of spring framing a favorite view. The success of these details does not arise from a random "let's make it pretty" effort. Such qualities are integral to the conception, design, and construction of a project.

Consider a beautifully proportioned public building, at the top of a stair and sitting on a knoll overlooking town. It would seem to have all the elements of a design success. And it will if thoughtful details complete the picture. But imagine the building clad in vinyl siding rather than in brick. Imagine a grand stair with narrow and steep treads. Imagine the trees that framed the building being cut down. It is still the same building and setting, but probably not what you envisioned. Details! Similarly, a well-conceived master plan for a roadway does not truly come alive until the detail elements are selected—richly sculpted light posts, the gentle arc of an overpass, a guard wall of native stone. These are the elements so often threatened or lost on our historic roads.

RICH HISTORIC DETAILS MAY TAKE MANY DIFFERENT FORMS. CONSIDER THE STREAMLINED TOLL BOOTHS AT THE GOLDEN GATE BRIDGE IN SAN FANCISCO (1937). *Paul Daniel Marriott.*

It is the details that distinguish your historic road and make it unique. Research their history, inventory what you have, and seek substitute or replacement detail elements of equal quality.

"The Lights Are Much Brighter There..." ⎯⎯⎯⎯⎯⎯⎯⎯⎯⎯

The lighting of the nighttime sky has, without question, made our cities and communities safer and more livable. Yet how many of us ever ponder the quality of that nighttime light, both aesthetically and environmentally? From our largest cities to our smallest villages and all along the roads that connect them, an eerie orange-pink glow has consumed us from dusk to dawn. This bright light, known as high-pressure sodium, has become a favorite source of illumination. Why? It is inexpensive and long lasting. It also distorts colors and shrouds light fixtures with a glare so powerful that it often obscures the design of the fixture itself.

For many historic roads, lighting was a carefully planned and thoughtfully selected detail element. These roads were often bathed in the warm light of incandescent bulbs. Incandescent lighting (the type likely found in your favorite reading lamp) casts a warm, true light with a minimum of glare. It enables you to enjoy the shape of a historic light globe rather than appearing as a fuzzy mass of pink light. Try observing it yourself. Look at a historic light fixture with sodium lighting during the day, and then at night. Notice how the details get lost? Now find a similar fixture with an incandescent bulb. The details present themselves warmly illuminated from the interior—the crisp white light illuminating the surrounding vegetation and pavement.

INCANDESCENT LIGHTING ALONG SPEER BOULEVARD, DENVER, 1910. *Colorado Historical Society.*

Washington, D.C. still uses incandescent lighting around the city's monumental core and in many residential neighborhoods. San Francisco also lights many streets with incandescent lighting. And Boston still lights much of historic Beacon Hill and the Back Bay with gas lights!

Isn't Preservation Expensive?

Yes and no. The cost of preservation, the reality of shrinking budgets, and the difficulty of raising funds will all be cited as you investigate the preservation of your historic road. Like safety, cost is a powerful argument to overcome. In order to be prepared for the inevitable cost questions, you need to prepare yourself with some equally strong arguments and solutions.

THE RESOURCE IS WORTH IT

You may think that stating "the resource is worth it" is an oversimplification of the obvious, but remember your audience. Even if you have managed to convince the public and the road manager that safety can be addressed, that still does not mean that you have convinced them of the value of the resource.

In a pleasant and nonargumentative way, explain the rich history of the route. Allow your enthusiasm for the road to come through. Help to instill in the community and decision makers a pride in the historic road, an awareness of the distinctive quality it brings to the community, and an affirmation of past glories. Whenever possible, point out the quality-of-life contributions a historic road makes. If the beauty of the route is one of the qualities that enhances your community, it may be helpful to question what its loss would do to that quality of life—loss of history, aesthetic experience, recreational space, tourism dollars, and perhaps *property values.*

You may also be able to appeal to your community's sense of responsibility. Doesn't the community have the responsibility to maintain and protect such significant resources?

Yes, preservation can cost money, but that expense does carry with it significant benefits. Remember, investments, such as lighting and stonework, are amortized over a period of many years. It may be to your benefit to cite expenses in extra cost per year over the life of the construction rather than as a large up-front cost.

PRESERVATION MAY BE CHEAPER

The most frequent threat to historic roads comes from a transportation department or office desiring to make changes to the roadway for safety. While realignment, widening of the roadway, and reconstruction of bridges can run into the millions of dollars, there is usually federal and state money available for such construction projects. In fact, it is often the availability of federal funds, more than needed construction, that drives such projects. You need to return to your original investigation of the historic road and safety issues to determine if such alterations seem appropriate. If the project represents an excessive endeavor championed by the state DOT, for example, you may be able to argue for basic repairs and modifications without sacrificing the historic integrity of the road. Obviously, this will be a less expensive solution. If you advance this idea in the appropriate manner, you may offer the state DOT the opportunity to abandon the construction project, having spent less of the taxpayer's money as well as appearing more favorable and fiscally responsible in the eyes of the public.

Super (elevation) Sunday

A difficult curve on the Bronx River Parkway in New York State was becoming a source of concern for the local DPW. The tight radius of the curve had been a source of accidents—drivers traveling at excessive rates of speed were ending up in the Bronx River. To solve this problem and thereby enhance safety and reduce tort liability, the county planned a $5 million realignment of the road to eliminate the curve. The realignment would rechannel the Bronx River and obliterate between a quarter and a half mile of Garth Woods, a wooded reservation from the 1906 parkway plan.

While touring the parkway on a bike one Sunday afternoon, a visiting engineer suggested the safety problem could be solved simply by stabilizing the parkway's shoulders, banking the curves (superelevation), and resurfacing with a skid-resistant pavement. The young man's comments made their way to the DPW, and within a few weeks the recommendations had been implemented for a mere $385,000. In this win-win situation, the historic character of the parkway was maintained, and the safety of the parkway was enhanced—all at minimal expense. Who says historic preservation doesn't pay?

≈

Preservation May Be Wiser

In those circumstances where preservation is more expensive, it may have long-term economic benefits. The solid construction practices of the past yielded structures and surfaces that have survived much longer than their contemporary counterparts. While the repair, rehabilitation, or restoration of historic features sometimes may cost more than new construction alternatives, the result could be a considerably longer life span. Do a cost-benefit analysis to determine the real costs. A few extra dollars up front may generate significant savings in the future.

More and more communities are also realizing that historic preservation makes good business sense. Historic preservation creates more jobs than the same amount of new construction—in new construction roughly 50% of costs go to labor; for historic preservation that figure is between 60% and 70%.[8] An added benefit is that these labor dollars are more likely to be returned to the local economy. The global economy and advances in communication have enabled the quality of life issue to be a major player in location decisions in today's business world—would you rather drive along a leafy historic road to the office or along 12 lanes of asphalt? Heritage tourism—tourism based on the unique historic resources of a community—is the fastest growing segment of the tourism market, with such travelers spending an average of half a day more than the typical tourist, according to the Heritage Tourism Program of the National Trust for Historic Preservation. Real estate studies have demonstrated the valuable economic contribution to the community of trees that grace so many of our historic roads—enhancing property values by up to 30%.[9]

The Merritt Parkway ————————————————————

When a number of bridges on Connecticut's Merritt Parkway needed to be widened due to deterioration and safety concerns, the responsible parties determined that new construction modeled on the historic reinforced concrete arches that gracefully span the parkway would be more expensive than modern concrete beams and simulated arches—a false facade concealing an ordinary flat-deck bridge. Thus a determination was made to rebuild with simulated arches.

Fortunately for the parkway and the people of Connecticut, a savvy state transportation administrator discovered that the concrete beam and simulated arch construction (experimented with on a few bridges) was not significantly less expensive than a genuine concrete arch and that it had a much shorter life span than the historic (genuine arch) concrete construction. Concrete construction of the bridges, recreating the architectural detail for which the parkway bridges are famous, over time, was competitive with simulated arches. The bridges have been reconstructed in concrete as genuine arches.

CONSTRUCTION WORKERS WIDENING A BRIDGE ON CONNECTICUT'S
MERRITT PARKWAY TO ENHANCE SAFETY. WHEN COMPLIMENTED
REGARDING THE QUALITY OF THE WORK AND SENSITIVITY TO HISTORIC
PRESERVATION, ONE WORKER REPLIED PROUDLY, "WE HAVE TO... THIS IS
THE MERRITT."
Paul Daniel Marriott.

NEWLY COMPLETED CONCRETE WORK REPLICATING ORIGINAL FEATURES
OF A MERRITT PARKWAY OVERPASS.
Paul Daniel Marriott.

NOTES

1. See U.S. Preservation Commission Identification Project (there were 1,857 preservation commissions nationwide as of December 1992).

2. Informal opinion of March 27, 1995, by Carla J. Stovall, Attorney General of Kansas, Office of the Attorney General, 301 S.W. 10th Avenue, Topeka, Kansas 66612.

3. *Designing Safer Roads: Practices for Resurfacing, Restoration, and Rehabilitation,* Special Report 214, Transportation Research Board, Washington, D.C., 1987, p. 12, hereafter referred to as *Safer Roads.*

4. *Manual on Uniform Traffic Control Devices for Streets and Highways,* Washington, D.C.: Federal Highway Administration, 1988.

5. All statistics cited in this section are from *Traffic Safety Facts 1995: A Compilation of Motor Vehicle Crash Data from the Fatal Accident Reporting System and the General Estimates System,* U.S. Department of Transportation, National Highway Traffic Safety Administration, Washington, D.C., September 1996, hereafter referred to as *Traffic Safety.*

6. Major Media of the Southeast v. City of Raleigh, 621 F. Supp 1446, 1451 aff'd 792F.2d 1269 (4th Cir. 1986), cert denied, 107 S. Ct. 1334 (1987).

7. "Safety and Environmental Design Considerations in the Use of Commercial Electronic Variable Message Signing," FHWA/RD 80/1 (June 1980).

8. Rypkema, Donald D., *The Economics of Historic Preservation,* Washington, D.C.: National Trust for Historic Preservation, 1994, p. 14.

9. American Forests, *Building Greener Neighborhoods,* National Association of Homebuilders, 1995.

ZION–MT. CARMEL HIGHWAY, ZION NATIONAL PARK, UTAH.
Library of Congress, Historic American Engineering Record.

Chapter 4
THE AASHTO GREEN BOOK

This chapter provides a brief introduction to a very lengthy and complex document. The intent of this summary is to assist the historic roads advocate and preservation community in having a better understanding of the guidelines by which many transportation decisions are made. Those sections summarized herein contain items and opportunities that, given a responsive DOT and a legitimate resource, can have positive results for historic roads. (All references are from the 1994 Green Book, *A Policy on Geometric Design of Highways and Streets, 1994,* ©1995, published by the American Association of State Highway and Transportation Officials, Washington, D.C. (used by permission) hereafter referred to as the GB where citations are needed.)

∽ An Introduction to the Green Book

If you are involved with any roadway project, historic or modern, you will soon learn of the Green Book. The Green Book is a publication of AASHTO (pronounced "ash-tow")—The American Association of State Highway and Transportation Officials. The Green Book is the popular name for a publication titled: *A Policy on Geometric Design of Highways and Streets,* the Green Book contains the recommended policies that define the design of our nation's roadways. Everything from city curbs, residential cul-de-sacs, and posted speeds on our interstates to the design of rest areas, commercial intersections, and recreational roads is addressed. The Green Book is reviewed and updated if necessary every four or five years, the latest edition having been published in 1994.

The purpose of the Green Book is to recommend safe practices for the planning, design, and layout of roadways. For preservationists, the Green Book is most often encountered during the reconstruction or rehabilitation of a historic road.

The development of guidelines for safe design is time consuming and costly. How wide should a bridge be to be safe? Will a particular guardrail stop a vehicle that has skidded off the road (an *errant vehicle*)? What is the safest design for a curve on a road with traffic traveling at 65 mph? 25 mph? The expense to test and develop safe design recommendations for any single state or jurisdiction could be prohibitive. There is also the desire to ensure uniform safety throughout the United States—to have some standardization. AASHTO is a professional nonprofit organization that works to develop the answers to these and many other questions.

Composed of highway design professionals from across the nation, AASHTO has had the safety of the motoring public at the center of much of its research. Their recommended findings for safe roadway

CONSTRUCTION OF THE BRONX RIVER PARKWAY, WESTCHESTER COUNTY, NEW YORK, 1923.
Courtesy of the Westchester (N.Y.) County Archives.

design form the core of the Green Book. Unfortunately however, in recent years many state and local governments, courts, and members of the transportation community have held the AASHTO Green Book up as an inflexible and rigid document. This perpetuates the myth that there is no flexibility in the publication and that the safety of the motoring public cannot be accomplished in alternative manners. This use and interpretation of the Green Book by many in the transportation profession has made the book somewhat of a nemesis to the preservation community.

What must be remembered is that the Green Book *recommends* guidelines to the states and local governments for the design of roadways. No state or local jurisdiction is required to adopt these guidelines. However, almost every state and the majority of local governments have adopted the AASHTO guidelines in full or in part. In this book, the word *standard,* when appearing in an example, refers to an adopted state or local policy. Some states use the AASHTO guidelines in a very flexible manner, adapting the recommended guidelines to particular needs and projects. Others follow the guidelines rigidly with little consideration for the flexibilities that exist within the Green Book or the site-specific needs of a project. Such rigid adherence to the Green Book frequently comes from fear of lawsuits that might find the road management entity negligent if flexibilities even those in the Green Book, are used.

In addition to state and local use, the FHWA has adopted the AASHTO Green Book as policy for all federal roads and construction projects. *Any federal project or the use of any federal monies requires adherence to the guidelines in the Green Book for projects on the NHS.* For projects off the NHS, the AASHTO Green Book does not need to be followed. However, some approved state or local standard must be adhered to for federally funded projects off the NHS. As already noted, due to the expense and difficulty in developing standards, most state and local governments do adopt the AASHTO guidelines with few, if any, modifications. Unless your state or local jurisdiction can offer an alternative standard, it is likely the project's design will still be dictated by AASHTO guidelines. The benefit of the new NHS legislation is that an opportunity now exists, where one did not before, to develop and use alternative standards.

Exceptions to the Green Book guidelines can be sought for road projects exhibiting special circumstances—many park and historic roads have sought and been awarded such exceptions. Design exceptions will be discussed later in this book.

When referring to the AASHTO Green Book, never refer to the contents as design regulations or design standards. The Green Book simply endorses the information as recommended guidelines for design and construction. The information in the Green Book does not become a standard or regulation unless your state or local jurisdiction adopts it as policy.

~

The Green Book establishes a range of acceptable values for highway design. For example, the recommended width of a country lane should be between 5.4 and 7.2 meters (m) (roughly 18 to 24 feet).(GB, p. 422) Parallel parking lanes on a busy downtown street should be between 2.4 and 3.6 m (roughly 8 to 12 feet). (GB, p. 412) While many states and courts tend to hold the highest values as the benchmark for safety, it must be remembered that the entire range has been tested and found to provide an acceptable range of safety for varying circumstances. One of the primary reasons for recommending a range rather than a specific design solution is to accommodate the infinite site-specific conditions that present themselves in any project. One of these considerations is whether the site is a historic or cultural resource.

Please note that, while the AASHTO Green Book is generally referenced for the management of existing roads, it is designed for assisting in the construction of new roads or the major reconstruction of existing roads. In fact, many historic road construction projects are undertaken as RRR projects, not new construction. Therefore, it must be remembered that the values presented in the Green Book aim to provide acceptible levels of safety for new construction. AASHTO notes that the Green Book is "not intended as a policy for resurfacing, restoration, or rehabilitation (RRR) projects" (GB, p. xliii). For existing roads designed to different standards at different times, the AASHTO Green Book should be consulted as a reference by which any reasonable and feasible accommodations for safety may be made. The likelihood of any historic road, or even a road designed in the 1970s, meeting all the recommended guidelines in the 1994 edition is unrealistic. Further, the Green Book is an ever changing document reflecting the latest in technology and research. Standards promoted in the coming century will likely determine model highways of today to be antiquated.

In order to assist you in understanding the 1006 pages of the Green Book, this chapter directs your attention to those areas of the Green Book that offer specific language or represent situations commonly found surrounding the preservation of a historic road.

The outline in this chapter will present those areas of the Green Book that are sensitive to historic roads. These positive and supportive passages represent a small percentage of the design philosophy and guidance presented in this lengthy volume. The material is presented here to assist the historic roads advocate by providing access to the few qualifying statements that directly, or through liberal interpretation, suggest alternatives sympathetic to historic roads.

THE ARROYO SECO PARKWAY UNDER CONSTRUCTION.
California Department of Transportation, Headquarters Photography Unit.

Going Metric

In the AASHTO Green Book, all measurements are metric. The FHWA is now in the process of converting to the metric system for all highway design and specifications. For your reference, 1 meter (m) equals 3.28 feet or 39.37 inches; 1 kilometer (km) equals 0.621 miles (mi). The following chart lists several metric measurements and their U.S. conversions. The figures have been rounded to the nearest whole number.

METERS/FEET		KPH/MPH		MPH/KPH	
1 m	3.28 ft	1 KPH	0.62 MPH	1 mph	1.6 kph
10	39	10	6	10	16
50	164	20	12	20	32
100	328	40	25	35	56
500	1,640	60	37	45	72
1,000	3,280	80	50	55	88
5,000	16,400	100	62	65	105

The Green Book is comprised of the following chapters:

Chapter I	Highway Function
Chapter II	Design Controls and Criteria
Chapter III	Elements of Design
Chapter IV	Cross Section Elements
Chapter V	Local Roads and Streets
Chapter VI	Collector Roads and Streets
Chapter VII	Rural and Urban Arterials
Chapter VIII	Freeways
Chapter IX	At-Grade Intersections
Chapter X	Grade Separations and Interchanges

Chapters I through IV address the basic terminology and structure of road design and development. Chapters V through VII address specific functional classifications of roads. Chapter VIII addresses freeways. Though not a separate functional classification (freeways are normally classified as principal arterials), freeways do possess unique qualities and circumstances. Chapters IX and X address intersections.

What follows are sections of the AASHTO Green Book and interpretive text to assist you in understanding how such sections might pertain to the preservation of historic roads.

∽ *Foreword (GB, p. xliii)*

While the needs of historic roads are relatively unique, the nature of balancing conflicting needs within our highway system is not new. The Foreword recognizes this inherent aspect of design and development and outlines a broad philosophy to address such issues. While the ultimate preservation of historic roads may not be achieved through the language of the Foreword, it is always good to have the strong philosophical support such statements provide.

The Foreword states:

> The fact that new design standards are presented herein does not imply that existing streets and highways are unsafe, nor does it mandate the initiation of improvement projects. (GB, p. xliii)

THE NATCHEZ TRACE PARKWAY WILL BE 445 MILES LONG AND LINK NASHVILLE, TENNESSEE, WITH NATCHEZ, MISSISSIPPI, WHEN COMPLETED. THIS SECTION, NEAR JACKSON, MISSISSIPPI, IS THE OLDEST SECTION OF THE PARKWAY, BEGUN IN 1937 (PHOTO 1950). THE PARKWAY HAS BEEN DEVELOPED UNDER CHANGING DESIGN GUIDELINES FOR THE LAST 60 YEARS.
Natchez Trace Parkway, National Park Service.

The Foreword continues by referencing the flexibility that should be used when undertaking any project. This language has direct and positive applications to historic preservation projects. Note in particular the consideration of social, economic, and environmental impacts. The Foreword continues

> The intent of this policy is to provide guidance to the designer by referencing a recommended range of values for critical dimensions. Sufficient flexibility is permitted to encourage independent designs tailored to particular situations. Minimum values are either given or implied by the lower value in a given range of values. *The larger values within the ranges will normally be used where the social, economic, and environmental (S.E.E.) impacts are not critical.* (emphasis added) (GB, p. xliii)

⌁ *Chapter I—Highway Functions*

FUNCTIONAL RELATIONSHIPS (GB, P. 5)

A system of classifying roadways by the character of service they provide was developed by AASHTO in order that appropriate design and safety measures could be articulated for different types of roads. Functional classification is based on the nature of typical trips (distance) on a road type. An interstate route is a more likely choice for long-distance travel than a residential street. Thus, guidelines for an interstate highway differ from those recommended for a neighborhood street. Functional classification forms the basis for the recommended guidelines in the Green Book. The classification of a road within a particular category suggests that the application of guidelines from another, generally lower, functional classification is unsafe; for example, the use of recommended safety practices of a neighborhood street may not be acceptable for an interstate highway.

It is important to understand the functional classification given to a historic road. Frequently, preservationists may find that the "required" actions promoted by the managing agency may not parallel the road's functional classification. In other words, a highway official may tend to recommend a more stringent state standard, regardless of the functional classification.

Every road in every state should have a functional classification. A federal program in the 1970s worked to develop comprehensive classification in every state. Frequently, however, when historic roads advocates inquire about their road's classification, they are informed that no classification exists. This is unlikely. You may need to consult with the main office of the state DOT to learn the proper classification. A lack of clarity or a local roadway manager who does not know a road's functional classification can hamper your efforts to promote flexibility and creative solutions. In such instances you may want to question the application of standards based on *unknown* classifications. You should also compare the use of the road at the time it was classified to its use today (regional issues)—it is possible to change functional classifications. If, for example, a bypass has since reduced the volume of traffic on your historic road, it may be eligible for a lower classification and the greater flexibility such design guidelines bring. As with all things, be sure the functional classification of your historic road makes sense.

DEFINITIONS OF URBAN AND RURAL AREAS (GB, P. 9)

Functional classifications are divided into rural and urban areas.

There are four rural functional classifications. (GB, p. 10)

Rural Principal Arterial
Rural Minor Arterial
Rural Collector (Major Collector Roads and Minor Collector Roads)
Rural Local

There are four urban functional classifications. (GB, p. 13)

Urban Principal Arterial
Urban Minor Arterial
Urban Collector
Urban Local

Road Classifications

The following definitions, based on the Green Book, have been designed to assist you in understanding functional classifications.

FREEWAY

A freeway is limited-access highway with grade-separated interchanges, such as an interstate. Freeways are not considered a functional classification by AASHTO; however, their distinct features are specifically addressed in the Green Book. Freeways regulate the entrance and exit of traffic through a system of ramps. No abutting properties may have access to a freeway via driveways or other entrances (this is called a limited-access highway). Cross traffic is carried over or under the freeway by bridges with ramps providing the connection (this is referred to as a separated-grade or grade-separated interchange). Examples: the U.S. interstate system, the New Jersey Turnpike, the Baltimore-Washington Parkway.

THE ARROYO SECO PARKWAY CONNECTING LOS ANGELES WITH PASADENA IS AN EXAMPLE OF A FREEWAY. DEDICATED IN 1940, THE PARKWAY BECAME A PROTOTYPE FOR THE CALIFORNIA FREEWAY SYSTEM.
California Department of Transportation, Headquarters Photography Unit.

ARTERIAL

Arterials provide the principal high-volume and high-speed routes within communities and connecting communities. Rural arterials may link farming communities or cross mountains. *Urban arterials may be two or more lanes, may have a center median, and will likely have traffic signals at key intersections. These are the roads that are likely to be jammed at rush hour or during holiday shopping. In older communities they may be lined with commercial establishments; in new communities they may be lined with the rear walls and plantings of adjacent subdivisions and commercial properties (newer properties backing up against the highway helps to limit access). Examples: Wilshire Boulevard in Los Angeles, U.S. Route 1, the National Road (U.S. 40), Lakeshore Drive in Chicago, Route 66, and Broadway in New York.*

THE LINCOLN PARK EXTENSION OF LAKESHORE DRIVE ALONG CHICAGO'S GOLD COAST, SEEN HERE IN 1941, IS AN EXAMPLE OF AN ARTERIAL.
Courtesy Chicago Park District, Special Collections.

COLLECTOR

Collector roads and streets carry traffic between local roads and streets and arterials. Collectors can provide access to business and residential properties abutting the road. Examples: The main through street in a residential neighborhood, the principal route through an office park.

THE KENTMERE PARKWAY IN WILMINGTON, DELAWARE, DESIGNED BY FREDERICK
LAW OLMSTED, IS AN EXAMPLE OF A COLLECTOR.
Paul Daniel Marriott.

LOCAL

*Local roads and streets serve farms, residences, and abutting businesses. They carry a low
volume of traffic and are used primarily for local trips. Examples: A residential street, a
cul-de-sac, a country lane.*

An example of a local road, this residential court in Baltimore's Guilford neighborhood was designed by the Olmsted firm.
Paul Daniel Marriott.

Functional Classification as a Design Type (GB, p. 15)

If you are in a situation in which no formal functional classification has been articulated or there is a desire to change the existing classification, remember to consider not only the physical attributes of your road (lane width, alignment, horizontal and vertical curvature) but also the road's intended service (leisure driving or commercial route) to determine the proper classification. For example, a parkway may have wide sweeping lanes, limited access, and a broad median—the physical attributes of a freeway. Yet the parkway may have been designed for leisure travelers to appreciate the natural and scenic beauty of an area. AASHTO notes:

> The functional concept is important to the designer. Even though many of the geometric standards could be determined without reference to the functional classification, the *designer must keep in mind the overall purpose the street or highway is intended to serve.* (emphasis added) (GB, p. 16)

AASHTO's definition for functional classification is based on *access* and *mobility*—how easily you can get on the road, and how swiftly it will take you someplace. Remember, some historic roads have dedicated purposes other than access and mobility.

～ *Chapter II—Design Controls and Criteria*

INFORMATION HANDLING EXPECTANCY (GB, p. 46)

Expectancy refers to the familiarity or predictability drivers innately experience on different types of roads. For example, while driving on an interstate you would never expect to encounter an intersection with traffic signals and cross-traffic. Similarly, you have different expectations in the supermarket parking lot—you exercise certain cautions because you know from past experience that there might be a cart in the parking space you are about to whip into. Such expectations are based on predictability and past experience. Expectancy can be likened to the safety considerations for a city driver and country driver on the same country road. For the country driver the road is

THIS ENTRANCE RAMP ON THE MERRITT PARKWAY COUNTERS THE MODERN DRIVERS EXPECTANCY DUE TO THE LACK OF A MERGE AREA FOR ENTERING PARKWAY TRAFFIC. TO MAKE DRIVERS AWARE OF THIS NONEXPECTED SITUATION, THE CONNECTICUT DOT HAS INSTALLED STOP SIGNS TO ALLOW DRIVERS A MORE CAREFUL ENTRANCE.
Paul Daniel Marriott.

relatively safe, because part of the country driver's expectancy accounts for the possibility of a slow-moving farm vehicle around the next curve. For the city driver unaccustomed to such vehicles, the expectancy may be that of an open country road—free and open and without the congestion and the surprises he or she is accustomed to. Now imagine the city driver rounding a curve at harvest time and encountering a farm wagon.

The Green Book recognizes expectancy. "Expectancies are formed by the drivers' experience and training. Situations that generally occur in the same way, and successful responses to these situations are incorporated into the drivers' stores of knowledge."(GB, p. 46) Further, "reinforced expectancies help drivers respond rapidly and correctly." (GB, p. 49) In other words, predictable environments provide the safest driving environments. Consider the chances of an unpredictable event on the interstate highway system compared to a commercial strip.

The Green Book continues by noting "unusual, unique, or uncommon situations that violate expectancies may cause longer response times, inappropriate responses, or errors." (GB, p. 49). How do you respond when speeding down an interstate, rounding a curve, and encountering stopped traffic due to an accident?

This section concludes by noting that "the production of designs in accordance with prevalent expectancies is one of the most important ways to aid performance. Unusual or nonstandard design should be avoided, and **design elements should be applied consistently throughout a highway segment.**" (emphasis added) (GB, p. 49) This comment is critical to both the safe operation of historic roads and the maintenance of their unique design. The irregular and inconsistent application of standards currently affecting historic roads is introducing elements and geometries that are often inconsistent with the expectancy of such roadways. The breakdown of design consistency generated by modifications along a historic road sends mixed signals to the driver and suggests responses to other driving experiences—the interstate, for example. Such conflicts cannot enhance safety.

For historic roads, expectancy is an important safety issue. If a historic road is consistent in its historic design, it establishes a driver expectancy. The winding roadway, overhanging trees, and stone bridges suggest an experience that is distinctly different from that of an interstate. Therefore, the driver will tend to respond differently by driving more slowly or exercising greater caution. Perhaps the lack of familiar jersey barriers (the angled concrete median barriers on many interstates), galvanized guardrail, or wide shoulders suggest that the route traveled is different from an interstate.

Now imagine that this historic road is going to have a central section straightened and widened with new shiny guardrail and bright lights at night. What do you think will happen? Very likely drivers in this rebuilt section will rely on their stores of knowledge and instinctively increase their speed due to the change in design. The rebuilt section will likely function effectively. What will happen at the point where the rebuilt section meets the historic section? Since the reconstructed segment will have created an *unusual or uncommon situation,* altering driver expectancy, drivers will suddenly brake or try to continue driving at high speeds as they reenter on the historic section. AASHTO notes that such situations are likely to increase driver error. So, what began as an initiative to improve safety on one segment of a historic road has the potential to actually diminish the overall safety on the route.

Driver Error (GB, p. 49)

Historic roads, like all roads, have their share of accidents involving drivers operating their vehicles under the influence of drugs or alcohol. It is important when addressing the safety issues surrounding a historic road to determine if the accidents are caused primarily by driver error or by deficiencies in the road's design. With regard to driver errors caused by alcohol, drugs, or fatigue, AASHTO notes:

> It is generally not possible for a design or operational procedure to reduce errors caused by innate driver deficiencies. (GB, p. 50)

The Pedestrian, General Considerations (GB, p. 97)

While this section is brief, it does acknowledge that pedestrians should be taken into consideration. You should note that some years

AN ACCIDENT ON THE BRONX RIVER PARKWAY, 1926.
Courtesy of the Westchester (N.Y.) County Archives.

pedestrian fatalities have accounted for between 7,000 and 8,000 of the approximate 40,000 highway deaths per year—a figure approaching 20% of the total fatalities.[1] (The figures for 1995: 5,585 pedestrian fatalities of the 41,798 overall traffic-related fatalities, 13.4% of the total.) Since some historic roads—urban boulevards or park roads, for example—have pedestrian components, it may be of value to know the AASHTO language.

> Pedestrians are a part of the everyday roadway environment, and attention must be paid to their presence in rural as well as urban areas. The urban pedestrian, being far more prevalent, more often influences roadway design features than the rural pedestrian does. Because of the demands on vehicular traffic in congested urban areas, it is often extremely difficult to make adequate provisions for pedestrians. *Yet this must be done,* because pedestrians are the lifeblood of our urban areas, especially in the downtown and other retail areas. (emphasis added) (GB, p. 97)

SAFETY (GB, P. 105)

The issue of safety is of paramount importance. It must be addressed by the preservation community in order to advance the preservation of historic roads. The purpose of this book is to suggest that there are alternate methods of providing safety; that an inflexible view toward safety solutions advanced by some state DOTs in certain instances lessens safety; and that environmental and experiential factors can and do influence safety.

The Green Book's strong safety focus is directed by a mandate from the U.S. Congress. Addressing highway safety in 1973, the House Committee on Public Works published the following statement included in the Green Book:

> Whose responsibility is it to see that maximum safety is incorporated into our motor vehicle transportation system? On this, the subcommittee is adamant. It is the responsibility of government and specifically those agencies that, by law, have been given that mandate. This responsibility begins with the Congress and flows through the Department of Transportation, its Federal Highway Administration, the State Highway Departments and safety agencies, and the street and highway units of counties, townships, cities and towns. There is no retreating from this mandate, either in letter or in spirit. (GB, p. 105)

This is strong language and a compelling force behind many of the decisions made regarding all roads, not just those that are historic. The preservation community cannot ignore this mandate and argue preservation simply for the sake of preservation. The preservationist must learn to look for new and creative ways in which safety can be both properly assessed and accommodated in a historic environment.

The Green Book continues in this section to note that accidents seldom result from a single cause. It notes that there are three groups of influences that affect an accident: the human element, the vehicle element, and the highway element. The key to safety, AASHTO argues, is a reduction in the number of decisions a driver must make. "Standardization in highway design features and traffic control devices plays an important role in reducing the number of required decisions; by this means, *the driver becomes aware of what to expect on a certain type of highway."* (emphasis added) (GB, p. 106)

When looking at historic roads, consider the standard that reduces decision making and promotes preservation objectives. This, of course, is very similar to the arguments made regarding expectancy.

The Clear Zone (GB, p. 110)

Of concern for many historic roads advocates are the recommendations for clear zones to create a forgiving roadside — a roadside in which a vehicle that strays from the roadway will not encounter hazards, thereby giving the driver the opportunity to regain control of the vehicle and return to the road. When many historic roads were established, the provision of a clear zone was not considered. Often structures and plant materials were located within areas that, under current recommendations, would remain clear. Many historic structures, significant trees, and natural features such as rock outcroppings within this zone have been destroyed or are facing destruction along historic roads. Many others have been encased by guardrails or other protective measures that have seriously altered historic detail and scale. While these changes have been responses to legitimate safety concerns in some instances, frequently, however, they have been the

GALVANIZED STEEL W BEAM, THE MOST COMMON GUARDRAIL.
Paul Daniel Marriott.

result of policy based on the local interpretation of the Green Book standards where there have been no demonstrated safety problems. Additional information on clear zones is available in AASHTO's *Roadside Design Guide* (1996).

The safety section closes with a commentary on billboards.

> Advertising or other roadside signs should not be placed where they would interfere with or confuse the meaning of standard traffic control devices. Advertising signs with bright colors or flashing lights are especially objectionable in this respect. Lights shining toward a driver can be blinding, partially or fully, for various periods, depending on individual eye capability. Bright lights, in effect, can form a curtain hiding what is ahead and thus endanger motorists and pedestrians. (GB, p. 112)

Chapter III—Elements of Design

HORIZONTAL ALIGNMENT (GB, P. 141)

Horizontal alignment refers to the degree of curvature a road has—how much it may curve to the left or the right. (Curvature regarding topography—the movement up and down over hills—is referred to as vertical alignment.) Frequently historic roads have curves that may be sharper or tighter than recommended for today, and this often leads to proposals and plans to straighten historic roads. Addressing the safety considerations horizontal alignment may initiate is often the first challenge a historic roads advocate faces.

Regarding the proposed straightening of a historic road, the advocate must determine what the root cause of the straightening proposal is. Do the curves on the historic road have a history of accidents? Or does the transportation agency simply desire to have a straighter road? AASHTO notes that the particulars of an individual roadway must be addressed. "For balance in highway design all geometric elements should, as far as economically feasible, be determined to provide safe, continuous operation *at a speed likely under the general conditions for that highway or street.*" (emphasis added) (GB, p. 141) In other words, be sure that the transportation agency is propos-

HORIZONTAL ALIGNMENT—THE DEGREE OF CURVATURE A ROAD HAS—
ALONG THE NATCHEZ TRACE PARKWAY IN TENNESSEE.
Natchez Trace Parkway, National Park Service.

ing a change or modification appropriate to the historic road in question and not a standard interstate-style response. Again, verify the functional classification of the road. What are the intended speeds and the intended use of the road as originally designed, and what are those of the proposed straightening?

General Considerations — Superelevation (GB, p. 142)

Superelevation refers to the banking of a curve such as those curves at an auto racetrack. This banking allows automobiles to navigate a sharper curve at higher speeds—the road slope, in a sense, pushes against the car's natural desire to fly out and away on a curve. In reality, superelevation is an everyday highway feature found on almost every curve on every interstate highway and on many secondary roads. Superelevation reduces or prevents the need for braking or slowing as a driver enters a curve, thus maintaining a more constant speed along the road. Though less exaggerated than its racetrack cousin, it functions in the same way.

For some historic roads, the installation of superelevation may be sufficient to increase the safety of historic horizontal alignment without the need for realignment of the road. Such a solution not only preserves the integrity of the original design, it is also economically prudent. Since superelevation was not a standard in highway engineering when many historic roads were designed and built, it represents one of the many resources that may assist in both the provision of a safe driving environment and the preservation of historic resources.

General Controls for Horizontal Alignment (GB, p. 223)

The Green Book acknowledges a number of general controls for horizontal alignment that "are not subject to empirical or formula derivation, but they are important for efficient and smooth-flowing highways." (GB, p. 223) The book notes, for example, that "excessive

THE HISTORIC COLUMBIA RIVER HIGHWAY, OREGON.
Paul Daniel Marriott.

curvature... causes economic losses because of increased travel time and operating costs, and *detract from a pleasing appearance.*" (emphasis added) (GB, p. 223) There are two things the historic roads advocate should be aware of regarding the basic philosophy behind these comments. First, many historic roads, particularly parkways, were not designed for efficiency of speed and movement, but for leisure travel. Second, what is the definition of *excessive curvature?* From this citation we might erroneously conclude that the sinuous Skyline Drive and the historic Columbia River Highway do not possess a pleasing appearance.

The section continues by listing nine general controls for road design. Numbers one and three, the most applicable to historic roads, are summarized here.

1. "Alignment should be as directional as possible but should be *consistent with the topography and with preserving developed properties and community values.*" (emphasis added) (GB, p. 224) Consider a historic landscape affiliated with an historic road as a developed property. Carefully designed landscapes with plantings, views, and structures are as "built" as a subdivision or shopping center—it is not vacant land awaiting highway realignment. The historic landscape provides the context for the road and reflects community values.

3. "Consistent alignment should always be sought. Sharp curves should not be introduced at the ends of long tangents. Sudden changes from areas of flat curvature to areas of sharp curvature should be avoided." (GB, p. 224) This statement supports the idea of maintaining the integrity of a winding historic road. Frequently, incremental changes alter one segment of a historic road for higher speed and straighter travel. The sudden changes that occur when historic road meets the new alignment can pose a safety hazard.

∿ *Chapter IV—Cross Section Elements*

LANE WIDTHS (GB, P. 333)

The AASHTO Green Book comments that "no feature of a highway has a greater influence on the safety and comfort of driving than the width and condition of the surface." (GB, p. 333) The Green Book

RECOMMENDED LANE WIDTHS HAVE CHANGED THROUGHOUT THIS CENTURY. THIS 9-FOOT PAVED STRETCH OF ROUTE 66, SOUTH OF MIAMI, OKLAHOMA, REPRESENTED THE ULTIMATE IN COMFORT AND TRAVEL WHEN OPENED C. 1930. *National Historic Route 66 Federation.*

notes that lane widths are commonly between 2.7 and 3.6 m (8 ft 10 in. and 11 ft 9 in.). The book further notes that, while "lane widths of 3.6m are desirable on both rural and urban facilities, *there are circumstances that necessitate the use of lanes less than 3.6m wide.*" (emphasis added) (GB, p. 335) Here the argument can again be made that preservation is one such circumstance.

When addressing lane width on an historic road, determine the issues that have prompted a potential widening. Once again, are the proposed changes safety related or policy related? Compare existing lane widths to the original or historic lane width. There are instances where a historic road originally had a generously proportioned single lane in each direction that was divided into two narrower lanes at a later date to increase automobile carrying capacity. In many areas, faced with increased demand, in other words, increased volume, such pavement striping to accommodate additional lanes has become common. Under such a scenario, it is regrettable that the road is being criticized and threatened because of narrow lanes when an administrative decision altering its original design is at the root of the problem.

SHOULDERS (GB, P. 335)

A shoulder refers to the surface immediately adjacent to and parallel to the travel lanes. It may or may not be surfaced. The purpose of the shoulder is to provide space for emergency stopping and to assist in stabilizing the roadbed.

The Green Book is fairly adamant regarding shoulder widths and recommends a width of 3.0 m (9.8 ft) as the normal shoulder on all high-type facilities (high speed and high volume). A minimum shoulder width of 0.6 m (2 ft) is recommended for all roads. For historic roads, the following language may be of assistance. "Although it is desirable that a shoulder be wide enough for a vehicle to be driven completely off the traveled way, narrower shoulders are better than none at all."(GB, p. 338) The Green Book further notes "narrow shoulders and intermittent shoulders are superior to no shoulders." (GB, p. 339)

A TYPICAL SHOULDER.
Paul Daniel Marriott.

SHOULDER CONTRAST (GB, P. 343)

The Green Book notes that "it is desirable that the color and texture of shoulders be different from those of the through-traffic lanes." (GB, p. 343) Fewer and fewer states contrast shoulder color, preferring instead to pave the shoulder in the same material as the travel lanes and delineate it with a white stripe. For historic roads forced to accommodate a shoulder, the contrast recommendation can assist in reducing the negative visual impact a shoulder may have. An alternate color can help to blend the shoulder into the landscape. In fact, AASHTO further notes that "various types of stone aggregates and *turf* offer good contrast." (emphasis added) (GB, p. 343) This minor reference does suggest that a stabilized vegetated shoulder is one acceptable option for shoulder design.

HORIZONTAL CLEARANCE TO OBSTRUCTIONS (GB, P. 344)

The provision of a *clear zone*—an area free of features such as trees, rock outcroppings, or structures (elements AASHTO calls *obstructions* or *obstacles*) alongside the travel lanes—helps to minimize the hazard to a vehicle that leaves the road—an errant vehicle. Regarding the concept of the clear zone, AASHTO notes: "The term 'clear zone' is

DETAIL—A STABILIZED VEGETATED SHOULDER ON THE COLONIAL PARKWAY IN VIRGINIA. AN AGGREGATE MIXTURE PROVIDES THE NEEDED STABILITY OF A SHOULDER WHILE ALLOWING GRASS TO GROW.
Paul Daniel Marriott.

used to designate the unobstructed, relatively flat area provided beyond the edge of the traveled way." AASHTO further notes that the "traveled way **does not** include shoulders or auxiliary lanes." (emphasis added) (GB, p. 344) This is important to remember because

THE STABILIZED VEGETATED SHOULDER, ONCE ESTABLISHED, IS VIRTUALLY INDISTINGUISHABLE FROM OTHER LAWN AREAS. THE SHOULDER HAS IMPROVED THE SAFETY OF THE COLONIAL PARKWAY WITHOUT DESTROYING ITS INTEGRITY THE WAY A TYPICAL SHOULDER WOULD HAVE.
Paul Daniel Marriott.

A NEWLY CREATED CLEAR ZONE ALONG THE GLENN HIGHWAY IN ALASKA.
Paul Daniel Marriott.

many transportation agencies measure the clear zone from the edge of the shoulder rather than from the edge of the traveled way. This careful distinction can help to save a few feet of clearance along a historic road if the clear zone includes the shoulders rather than being measured from the edge of the shoulder.

Developing a clear zone on a historic road can result in the destruction or alteration of roadside details such as historic walls or fences; it can also result in the clear-cutting of all trees within the area.

For low-speed rural collectors and rural local roads, AASHTO recommends a clear zone of 3.0 m (9 ft 10 in.). For higher-speed roads, the AASHTO *Roadside Design Guide* determines clear zones by speed, volume, and side embankment. Because many transportation agencies recommend a flat 30-ft clear zone in almost all situations, it is wise to consult the AASHTO publication to determine the appropriate width for a recommended clear zone.

Traffic Barriers (GB, p. 361)

This section outlines the general circumstances in which barriers are recommended. Traffic barriers are generally recognized as guardrails or jersey barriers. While the section offers little information for the historic roads advocate, it does acknowledge that "barriers are a source of accident potential themselves." The section further notes that "short lengths of roadside barriers are discouraged." (GB, p. 363)

The fact that barriers may be a potential cause of accidents themselves should not be construed to mean that barriers are unnecessary. In certain instances where the installation of barriers actually increases the accident rate, if the barriers reduce the number of more serious accidents or fatalities, their use will be justified. An increase in fender benders is generally considered an acceptable trade-off for reduced fatalities.

There are several new barrier designs that are more sympathetic to historic roads. Wood rails with a steel backing, stone walls with a hidden concrete core, concrete walls that look like stone, and others are currently approved for use on our nation's highway system. **See Appendix B** for a listing of several approved barriers.

Note: Chapters V through VIII refer to specific functional classifications. You may wish to reference your historic road's functional

THE DUMBARTON BRIDGE, COMPLETED IN 1915, OVER ROCK CREEK AND
POTOMAC PARKWAY, WASHINGTON, D.C.
Paul Daniel Marriott.

THE BRIDGE WALLS ON THE DUMBARTON BRIDGE DO NOT MEET MODERN CRASH
REQUIREMENTS. RATHER THAN OBSCURING THE HISTORIC SANDSTONE WALLS WITH
JERSEY BARRIERS OR GUARDRAIL, A BOX BEAM WAS LOCATED ALONG THE CURB.
Paul Daniel Marriott.

NOT ONLY DOES THE BOX BEAM BARRIER PREVENT AN ERRANT VEHICLE FROM
KNOCKING A PORTION OF THE STONE WALL TO THE PARKWAY BELOW; IT ALSO
PROVIDES ADDITIONAL SAFETY FOR THE PEDESTRIAN.
Paul Daniel Marriott.

classification, or its characteristics if no functional classification has
been clearly articulated, before proceeding. However, all the language
selected from these chapters can benefit historic roads, so you will
want to familiarize yourself with as much of the information as possible.

⌒ Chapter V — Local Roads and Streets

Chapter V of the AASHTO Green Book applies to roads that are
functionally classified as local rural roads and local urban streets. In
general, the recommended guidelines can be applied to village or city
streets, as well as township and county roads. The following sections
are applicable to the historic roads advocate.

LOCAL RURAL ROADS (GB, P. 418)

Local Rural Roads, Bridges to Remain in Place (GB, p. 423)

With regard to historic structures, in particular historic bridges,
AASHTO presents a fairly liberal view regarding such structures on
local rural roads.

Existing substandard structures should be improved, but because of their high replacement cost, reasonably adequate bridges and culverts that meet tolerable criteria may be retained. Some non-technical factors that should be considered are the *aesthetic value and historical significance* attached to famous structures, covered bridges, and stone arches." (emphasis added) (GB, p. 423)

Local Urban Streets (GB, p. 429)

For the purposes of this book, the information on local urban streets will be of greatest value to historic community streets, or streets within an historic district. In many instances, communities are discouraged from locating trees, lighting, and other amenities alongside the road. In other places, DOTs assert the need to remove trees lining the streets of historic communities due to the obstacles they are perceived to present. As always, check the functional classification of the road to determine what guidelines you will be up against.

Local Urban Streets, Horizontal Clearance to Obstructions (GB, p. 438)

On local urban streets, a minimum clearance of 0.5 m (1 ft 7 in.) is recommended between the face of the curb and fixed structures such as light standards, fire hydrants, and utility poles. Trees are considered minimal hazards along local streets with barrier curbs (a curb with a vertical face, unlike a mountable curb with a rolled face which allows an automobile to mount more easily) and speeds lower than 60 kph (37 mph).

Local Urban Streets, Border Area (GB, p. 438)

The border area is the area between the roadway and the right-of-way. It is provided to enhance the safety of both motorists and pedestrians. Typically, the border area is where you would find street trees, lighting, benches, and other outdoor furniture. The Green Book notes "the *preservation and enhancement* of the environment is of major importance in the design and construction of local streets." (emphasis added) (GB, p. 438)

RECREATIONAL ROADS (GB, P. 443)

Because of language strongly supporting the distinctive needs of recreational roads, the introductory paragraphs to this section are presented here in full.

> Roads serving recreational sites and areas are unique in that they are also part of the recreational experience. Design criteria described herein meet the unusual requirements of roads for access to, through, and within recreational sites, areas, and facilities for the complete enjoyment of the recreationist. *The criteria are intended to protect and enhance the existing aesthetic, ecological, environmental, and cultural amenities that form the basis for distinguishing each particular recreational site or area.*
>
> Visitors to a recreational site need access to the general area, usually by a statewide or principal arterial highway. Secondly they need access to the site. This is the most important link in from the statewide road system. For continuity beyond this point, design criteria require that the visitor be made aware of the nature of the area. *The design should be accomplished by a multidisciplinary team of varied backgrounds and experience, to ultimately provide a road system that is an integral part of the recreation site.* Depending on the conditions, internal tributaries will have a variety of lower design features. (emphasis added) (GB, p. 443)

The criteria outlined in Chapter V are applicable for public roads within all types of recreational areas. Remember, Chapter V addresses the issues of local roads and streets, so the information presented for recreational roads should be construed to be applicable to recreational roads with design speeds under 60 kph (37 mph). Still, the strong language referencing natural and cultural resources and a multidisciplinary team could have broader applications to historic roads as a whole—even those with design speeds above 60 kph (37 mph) such as some of the later parkways.

Recreational Roads, Horizontal Alignment (GB, p. 448)

"Because the use of straight sections of roadway would be physically impractical and (for recreational roads) aesthetically undesirable, horizontal curves are necessary elements." (GB, p. 448)

TOUR BUSSES ENTERING MT. MCKINLEY NATIONAL PARK
(NOW DENALI NATIONAL PARK) IN THE 1930S.
Alaska State Library.

Recreational Roads, Widths of Traveled Way, Shoulder, and Roadway (GB, p. 449)

"The low operating speeds and relatively low traffic volume on recreational roads do not warrant wide shoulders. In addition, wide shoulders may be aesthetically objectionable." (GB, p. 449)

Recreational Roads, Clear Recovery Area (GB, p. 452)

"Providing a clear zone adjacent to a road involves a trade-off between safety and aesthetics. A driver who leaves the road should be provided a reasonable chance to regain control and avoid serious injury. On the other hand, the philosophy of recreational roads dictates that *natural roadside features be preserved* where possible." (emphasis added) (GB, p. 452)

Recreational Roads, Roadside Barrier (GB, p. 453)

Regarding the provision of roadside barriers, "The criteria used in freeway design do not fit the low-volume recreational road situation." (GB, p. 453)

~ Chapter VI—Collector Roads and Streets

RURAL COLLECTORS (GB, P. 460)

Rural Collectors, Design Traffic Volumes (GB, p. 460)

AASHTO recommends that rural collectors be designed for a level of service anticipated 20 years into the future. For many historic roads, it is a heavy burden to accommodate as yet unrealized traffic. In such circumstances, it is important to scrutinize the data supporting the traffic projections. Traffic prognostication, although mathematically based, relies on a number of speculations concerning land use and travel behavior. Projected traffic volume 20 years in the future, for example, is based on a series of assumptions that may change due to land development, economic stability, and regional growth patterns—even telecommuting may factor into this process one day. The blind acceptance of these figures projecting traffic 20 years in the future further suggests the inability of a community to develop plans and policies to lessen traffic impacts, develop alternative strategies, or have a meaningful voice in its future.

Rural Collectors, Bridges to Remain in Place (GB, p. 466)

"Because of their high cost, reasonably adequate bridges and culverts that meet tolerable criteria should be retained." (GB, p. 466) Essentially, an existing bridge may remain when its structural capacity in terms of design loading—that is, the amount of weight the bridge can support—and the roadway width meet a minimum value (see Table VII-6, Minimum structural capacities and minimum roadway widths for bridges to remain in place [GB, p. 467]).

Rural Collectors, Horizontal Clearances to Obstructions (GB, p. 468)

On rural collectors with a design speed of 60 kph (37 mph) or less, AASHTO recommends a clear zone of 3.0 m (10 ft). Consult the AASHTO *Roadside Design Guide* for 80 kph (50 mph) and above.

Urban Collectors (GB, p. 470)

Urban Collectors, Parking Lanes (GB, p. 474)

AASHTO considers on-street parallel parking to represent a safety problem and an impediment to traffic flow (both due to the possibility of an individual pulling into the travel lane without properly checking for oncoming traffic). AASHTO does note, however, that "parallel parking lanes currently are conventional on many collector streets." (GB, p. 474) The Green Book recommends that parking lanes be from 2.1 to 3.0 m (6.9 to 9.8 ft) wide in residential areas and between 2.4 and 3.0 m (7.9 and 9.8 ft) in commercial areas. Diagonal or angle parking, common in many midwestern communities, is recommended only in special cases.

Urban Collectors, Horizontal Clearance to Obstructions (GB, p. 477)

On all urban collectors with curbs, AASHTO recommends a minimum clear zone of 0.5 m (1.6 ft). Where parking lanes are present, the recommendation is a minimum clear zone of 0.6 m (2.0 ft) to allow for opening car doors. Remember, street trees, lights, and benches are all considered obstacles. Regarding trees, AASHTO notes: "Other off-roadway obstacles such as trees that might seriously damage out-of-control vehicles should be removed from the roadside wherever feasible. *However, the potential benefits from the removal of trees should be weighed against the adverse effects that their removal may have on the roadside environment;* and they should be removed only when necessary for reasons of safety." (emphasis added) (GB, p. 477)

Urban Collectors, Border Area (GB, p. 478)

The border area is the area between the roadway and the right-of-way line. Interestingly, AASHTO notes that "traffic signals, utility poles, fire hydrants, and other utilities should be placed *as far back of the curb as practical* for safety reasons." (emphasis added) (GB, p. 479) The preceding section on horizontal clearances clearly identifies trees as obstacles and recommends their removal with a prescribed distance from the curb. Yet utilities are encouraged to be located away from the curb *if practical*. Again, there are subtle inconsistencies in how the Green Book may be interpreted. Is a fixed object such as a fire hydrant less of a dangerous obstacle than a tree?

Chapter VII—Rural and Urban Arterials (GB, p. 483)

The chapter on rural and urban arterials does not contain any specific language supportive of historic roads. The chapter addresses basic functional and design issues for arterials. However, you will still want to be familiar with its contents should you be addressing a historic road that carries a functional classification of rural or urban arterial.

Chapter VIII — Freeways

Freeways are defined as expressways with *full control of access*—in other words, access to the roadway by all abutting land owners is controlled. Private driveways, at-grade intersections, and service roads are accessible only through entrance and exit ramps.

Unless your historic road meets the AASHTO definition of a freeway (such as the Baltimore-Washington Parkway, the Merritt Parkway, and the Arroyo Secco Parkway), it should not be held to the recommended guidelines contained in Chapter VIII. Even then, these distinct historic parkways possess special characteristics and design intents that warrant flexibility and sensitivity in the application of the guidelines.

Chapter IX—At-Grade Intersections

Although this chapter on at-grade intersections (typical intersections where roadways meet or intersect on the ground) does not contain any specific language supportive of historic roads, you will still want to be familiar with its contents should you be addressing a historic road in which at-grade intersections have become an issue.

❧ Chapter X—Grade Separations and Interchanges

This chapter discusses grade separations (a vertical difference road-ways) and interchanges (intersections where one road passes over or under another) and does not contain any specific language support-ive of historic roads. However, you need to be familiar with its contents in case you are addressing a historic road that has grade separations and interchanges.

❧ Other AASHTO Guides

While the Green Book is the most extensive source of information regarding guidelines for the nation's roadways, there are other AASHTO publications that can be helpful as well.

A Guide for Transportation Landscape and Environmental Design
Roadside Design Guide
An Informational Guide for Roadway Lighting
Standard Specifications for Highway Bridges
Guide for Accommodating Utilities Within Highway Right-of-Way

---

The Green Book and other guides are available from

The American Association of State Highway and Transportation Officials (AASHTO)
   444 North Capitol Street, NW
   Suite 249
   Washington, DC 20001

❧

NOTES

1. *1995 Highway Statistics Report,* Federal Highway Administration.

MASSACHUSETTS AVENUE OVER ROCK CREEK AND POTOMAC PARKWAY,
WASHINGTON, D.C.
Jack Boucher.

Chapter 5
WHAT YOU
NEED TO DO

Once you have organized the issues and yourself, you must assemble the necessary information and data to advance the preservation of your historic road. You cannot approach your state DOT or local transportation department without credible documentation and research. Learn the specifics and ask questions. If you are working to preserve a historic road, you must ask yourself some serious questions, research the issues, determine the rationale behind proposed changes, and identify the players.

∼ Evaluate Your Historic Road

Now that you've had an introduction to the issues, policies, and realities surrounding historic roads, its time to review the questions you were first asked in Chapter 1. They are included here, along with additional questions that will assist you in better determining the needs and realities of your historic road.

DEFINING YOUR ROAD

1. Is your road historic?
   - Does it represent a significant period of design (a parkway, an early freeway, an urban boulevard)? In other words, is the physical design of the road (its alignment, interchanges, setting within the landscape) of historic significance?
   - Is it listed in, or eligible for listing in, the National Register of Historic Places?

- Does it represent a significant period of transportation (transcontinental route, colonial toll road), where the function of the road is more important than the design?
- Does it represent significant construction techniques or technologies?
- Are the original design features still in place (pavement, bridges, lighting, landscape, retaining walls)?
- Are there any social or cultural events that have influenced the road, or perhaps even inspired its construction (the interstate system, designed for wartime evacuation and defense movement, for example)?
- Are there any famous personalities associated with the route (a famous designer such as Frederick Law Olmsted or H.W.S. Cleveland, an explorer such as Juan Bautista de Anza, or an infamous association such as the escape route taken by John Wilkes Booth)?

QUINCY SHORE DRIVE, 1916, BOSTON METROPOLITAN PARK SYSTEM.
Courtesy Metropolitan District Commission Archives, Boston.

2. What type of historic road do you have? (From Chapter 2.)
   - Aesthetic route?
   - Engineered route?
   - Cultural route?
3. How is the road managed?
   - Is it managed by the federal, state or local government?
   - Is the road a part of the NHS?
   - What government entity is responsible for the liability of the road?
   - Are there multiple partners (the parks department maintaining the landscape and the DPW maintaining the road surface)?
4. What standards guide the management of the road?
   - Has the state or local government adopted the AASHTO-recommended guidelines as policy?
   - Does the state or local government use standards that were developed independently of the AASHTO guidelines?
   - Does the management entity have a history of applying for exceptions to design standards, or are standards rigidly adhered to regardless of expressed flexibilities or allowable ranges for potential solutions?
5. What is the functional classification of the road?
   - Are standards applicable to a specific functional classification being advocated when a different functional classification exists? (Consult Chapter 4 of this book or the AASHTO Green Book.)
6. Does the road have any current restrictions or prohibitions on its use?
   - Can only certain types of vehicles use the road (many parkways are limited to automobile use)?
   - Are there any weight or size limits?
   - Are limitations designed to protect the quality of the road experience (limiting commercial vehicles) or are they due to failing infrastructure (limiting vehicle weight on structurally poor bridges)?
   - Are vehicle restrictions accounted for in management decisions (a road limited to auto use being guided by policies that include the accommodation of trucks)?
   - How are these restrictions enforced? By whom? How well?

SOME THINGS NEVER CHANGE—TRAFFIC CONGESTION ALONG
THE BRONX RIVER PARKWAY IN 1922.
Courtesy of the Westchester (N.Y.) County Archives.

TRAFFIC CONGESTION ON INDEPENDENCE AVENUE ALONGSIDE WASHINGTON, D.C.'S
HISTORIC TIDAL BASIN, DEVELOPED AS PART OF THE MCMILLIAN COMMISSION PLAN
FOR WASHINGTON IN 1901.
Paul Daniel Marriott.

7. What is the nature of the traffic on your historic road?
    - What is the traffic volume of the road? Is the road handling volumes of traffic beyond its original capacity? If there are proposed changes, do they meet projected capacity needs or will the road still be over capacity?
    - Does traffic generally travel below, at, or above the posted speed limit?
    - Has the posted speed limit changed since the road first opened? How often and when?
    - If the speed limit did change, what motivated that change?
    - For what speed was the road originally designed?
8. Who pays for maintenance and upkeep of the road?
    - Does the historic road receive funding from the local, state, or federal government?
    - Are some funds used for specific types of work (for example, certain funds that are used exclusively for landscape maintenance)?
    - Are there any prohibitions against the use of matching or private funds for road projects?

DEFINING THE ISSUES FACING YOUR HISTORIC ROAD

9. Are there threats to the integrity of your historic road?
    - Is there a planned reconstruction or demolition that is insensitive to the road's special qualities ?
    - Does the managing agency (state DOT, local DPW, Highway Authority, and so on) understand the history and value of the resource?
    - Do the threats originate from ignorance, safety or liability pressures, or lack of financial resources?
    - Is a change in land use policy likely to increase traffic demand on the historic road in the coming decades?
    - Is there a larger-issue item—such as a planning agency desiring the completion of a master plan or an urban renewal scheme— that is directing a proposed action threatening the historic character of your historic road?
    - If there is a threat, who is providing the funding for the project? Who initiated the project?

10. If there are threats, how immediate are they?
    - Are the threats to your historic road imminent, in the planning stage, or envisioned by you as a realistic possibility in the coming years? In other words, are the bulldozers lining up, has a proposal to remove historic stone walls been put forth, or do you see a change in zoning doubling the traffic on the historic road 10 years from now?

11. Does the road have demonstrated safety problems?
    - Does the road have a high accident rate?
    - How does the accident rate compare to other roads in the region? To other roads performing similar functions in the region?
    - Does the road meet commonly accepted safety standards?

12. If there have been previous alterations to the historic road for safety, have the changes enhanced the safety of the route?
    - Did changes reduce the accident rate?
    - Did changes increase the accident rate?
    - Did the change cause an increase in the number of accidents on another part of the road?
    - Were the changes sympathetic to the historic design?
    - Did driver behavior improve or worsen (did drivers begin driving faster or more slowly)?

13. Are existing local or state standards applied consistently?
    - Does the management entity insist on cutting down all the trees in the clear zone, yet allow utility poles to remain?
    - Do other roads in the state or region possess features or conditions not yet identified as problems, but judged unsatisfactory on your historic road?

RESPONDING TO SPECIFIC PROPOSED CHANGES OR THREATS

14. What policies are being cited regarding the proposed activity?
    - AASHTO guidelines, state policies, regional transportation projects?
    - A legal responsibility?
    - A requirement for a certain type of funding?

15. What are the accident statistics for the area in question?
    - How are accident statistics recorded?

- Are general accident statistics being cited (the overall statistics for the road) for a site-specific project? In other words, are the statistics cited relevant to the proposed activity?
- Are site-specific accident statistics (those at a bridge, for example) being cited to justify projects elsewhere ("It's only a matter of time before the same thing happens on this bridge.")?
- Is there a serious and legitimate accident problem on, or on a portion of, your historic road?

16. Have there been any previous efforts to enhance preservation or safety due to similar issues?
    - A project initiated for identical reasons 10 years ago?
    - If implemented, did the project accomplish the goals for which it was initiated (for example, did an accident rate go down)?

17. What sections of the AASHTO Green Book, if any, are being referenced for this project?
    - If referenced, is the appropriate functional classification being cited?
    - Are there any flexibilities within cited sections that are not being acknowledged?

18. What outside experts can offer you technical assistance or provide you with letters of support or documentation regarding your historic road?
    - Preservationists?
    - Engineers?
    - Landscape Architects?

You would be surprised how many road projects are undertaken due to policy but without substantive documentation. "The road is too narrow, therefore it is unsafe." Based on what? Frequently it is based on little more than recommended guidelines. The road may have the lowest accident rate in the state. You may find, by asking a few simple questions, that there is little basis for the destruction of your historic road.

---

19. Are federal or state funds being used for this project?
    - Determine all the funding sources for the project.
    - Will funding be lost if it is not used, or can it be applied to other projects?

20. Have the required Environmental Impact Statement (EIS) or Environmental Assessment (EA) been prepared?
    - Have all federal or state requirements (Section 106 or EIS procedures, for example) been met?
    - Have historic resources affected by the road project been fully and properly identified to determine their significance and the anticipated effect of the project?
    - Has the public review and comment requirement been implemented?

DEFINING AN APPROPRIATE COURSE OF ACTION

21. What do you hope to accomplish?
    - Complete preservation of the historic road?
    - Minor changes to the road for safety or other needed modifications, if designed and executed in a manner responsive to the historic design and integrity of the resource?
    - Increased awareness of the value of the historic route?
22. What specific actions will be needed to accomplish your goals?
    - A master plan or corridor management plan?
    - Increased community awareness?
    - Accident rate studies? Historic resource inventories?
    - Funding sources?
    - Will you need outside assistance to accomplish your goals?
23. What other key players are involved, directly or indirectly, in decisions regarding your historic road?
    - Who are the local, state, and federal elected officials whose districts include the historic road?
    - Is there a local, regional, or state historic preservation agency or group?
    - Is the SHPO familiar with the history and needs of historic roads in your state (the SHPO will be required to comment on a project if the road is listed in the National Register or DOE and federal funds are being used)?
    - Does the community support the preservation of the road?
    - Does the community recognize the value of the route?

- Does a proposed alteration or destruction of historic resources offer other benefits (real or perceived) to the community at large, such as a faster commute to work?

24. What resources do you have?
    - Do you have any original plans—engineering, structural, landscape?
    - Are there any records documenting land acquisition for the project?
    - Do you have any historic newspaper articles, photographs, or films of the road?
    - Do you have any current research papers or articles on the road?
    - Do you have a good map of the route?

25. When is compromise acceptable and when is it not?
    - You must be willing to compromise.
    - Are there changes that could improve the safety of the road without compromising its historic integrity?
    - What activities or changes would destroy the integrity of the road?

∾ *Determine the Rationale*

IS THE RATIONALE BEHIND THE THREAT OR ISSUE LEGITIMATE?

The four threats (realignment, destruction, replacement, and regional threats) are generally prompted by the three issues identified in Chapter 3—safety, liability, and ignorance. You must now evaluate your threats as articulated and make a determination as to which single issue or combination of the three issues is motivating the proposed changes to your historic road. Be honest. There are likely to be instances in which the actions you view as a threat to preservation are generated by the legitimate concerns of others. For example, is safety being argued due to demonstrated problems, such as a high accident rate. If you ignore legitimate safety issues or deny their existence in the face of supportive evidence, you will jeopardize your credibility and your chances of preserving the historic road.

Determine whether the rationale is legitimate or not. You may wish to solicit the advice or technical opinion of a professional preservationist or transportation expert knowledgeable about preservation. Trust your judgment—if you have a slight hesitation regarding the proposed changes or alteration of your historic road, it is likely that further investigation is needed.

Yes, The Rationale Is Legitimate

If you determine that the rationale behind the proposed projects is legitimate, you still have many options available to you. You must remember, however, that your argument is not against the action but in how the action will be implemented. Legitimate rationale will challenge you to identify the creative solutions and compromises addressing the issue and championing preservation.

THE COLORADO STREET BRIDGE IN PASADENA, CALIFORNIA, WAS RECENTLY RETROFITTED FOR SEISMIC CONCERNS. THE WORK, CARRIED OUT WITH A SENSITIVITY TO THE HISTORIC FEATURES OF THE BRIDGE, SHOULD ENABLE THE STRUCTURE TO SURVIVE AN EARTHQUAKE BETTER. THIS IS AN EXAMPLE OF LEGITIMATE RATIONALE. *Paul Daniel Marriott.*

No, The Rationale Is Not Legitimate

If there appears to be no logic or pressing need behind the proposed action, it will be your task to argue against the action. Determine the origin or inspiration for the action—safety considerations, liability, or ignorance. In other words, is the proposed widening of a historic road viewed as a tool to enhance safety? It is possible too that the proposed action is part of a larger plan to *upgrade* roads, or that there is funding for certain types of road *improvements.* Even without a demonstrated safety need, the management entity may perceive such actions as safety enhancements. Identify the facts or figures, if any, justifying the proposal. Keep in mind, professionals do not like to be told that they misunderstand their own resources. Savvy communication skills will be important. If that doesn't work, arguing the unnecessary expenditure of public funds can be effective.

Language

The language of the engineering community may subtly direct or sway public opinion in favor of certain transportation goals. For example, road construction projects are generally referred to as improvements *or* upgrades *in service. Are they? Trees and historic lighting may be referred to as* obstacles. *A fair characterization for a 70-year-old oak? As a historic preservation advocate, you may want to refer to improvements such as road construction projects as* alterations *or* destructions. *Furthermore, you might refer to the trees and lights as* contributing historic resources *or* quality-of-life elements.

WHAT IS THE PRESERVATION ISSUE?

How strong the issue of historic preservation should be in your arguments and strategies to save your historic road will vary. You will want to address context and integrity, rationale, the history of the road, and its use—both historic and contemporary. There are essentially two stagies you can follow regarding the preservation of your historic road: preservation-based and project-based.

Preservation-based Strategies

Strategies to preserve and protect historic roads based strongly on historic preservation will apply to routes that have a significant history of design, development, or technology associated with the road and its landscape. Further, such routes should demonstrate a high level of context and integrity. Preservation arguments essentially say, "This road is historic and significant. Changes should not be made unless there is no viable or prudent alternative. Then, such changes should be made in a manner that is least intrusive on the historic design of the road."

Any change to an existing feature should be carefully considered. Will a proposed action destroy a significant and recognized example of design technology, a feature designed by a noted designer, or a planned experience such as views or interactions with the natural or urban landscape? The changing of historic alignment or widening of bridges could destroy significant artifacts. Preservation-based strategies will focus on these types of historic attributes in arguing the preservation of the road.

Project-based Strategies

Project-based strategies focus on unwarranted or excessive modifications to any road, such as widening for the sake of widening or new lights because funding was available, and address changes for historic

INTERSTATE 64 CROSSING THE 1930s COLONIAL PARKWAY IN VIRGINIA. THE TWIN BRICK BRIDGES, CONSTRUCTED IN THE 1970s, CARRYING INTERSTATE TRAFFIC REPLICATE THE HISTORIC BRIDGES CONSTRUCTED DURING THE NEW DEAL. NOW THAT THE TREES HAVE GROWN AROUND THE NEW BRIDGES, FEW PARKWAY TRAVELERS REALIZE THEY ARE PASSING UNDER A MAJOR INTERSTATE. *Paul Daniel Marriott.*

THE STRIKINGLY MODERN NATCHEZ TRACE PARKWAY VIADUCT (CONSTRUCTED 1996) CARRYING PARKWAY TRAFFIC OVER A PICTURESQUE TENNESSEE VALLEY, HAS A MINIMAL VISUAL IMPACT ON THE LANDSCAPE. UNLIKE THE I-64 BRIDGES ON THE COLONIAL PARKWAY, THE NATCHEZ TRACE DRIVER DOES NOT SEE THE BRIDGE STRUCTURE. THEREFORE A HISTORIC HEAVY-MASONARY SOLUTION WOULD HAVE GONE UNAPPRECIATED BY THE PARKWAY TRAVELER AND WOULD HAVE OBSCURED LONG VIEWS THROUGH THE VALLEY.
Federal Highway Administration.

roads that have been sufficiently degraded; in other words, roads low in context and integrity. In general, project-based strategies look more at the impact of an action on a specific location or feature, whereas preservation-based strategies assess the impact of the action on the entire resource.

Project-based strategies for historic roads are likely to address isolated remains along roads that have lost much of their original integrity. Such arguments may focus on the preservation of specific resources—a bridge or a stone wall, for example—that are significant locally. In such instances, a minor realignment or architecturally sensitive widening of a bridge may be acceptable so long as the overall character of the resource is not damaged.

PRESERVATION-BASED OR PROJECT-BASED?

For you to better understand how different road types determine different preservation solutions, three scenarios are presented here. For each of these three examples the issue will be the replacement of a curving section of a historic road with a newer, wider, straighter section.

Our first two situations concern the historic Columbia River Highway in Oregon.

Situation Number 1

If a proposal were made to straighten a section of the historically designed alignment due to *demonstrated safety* problems, this would initiate a preservation-based strategy. Due to the highway's historic alignment and advanced technology at the time of construction, altering the road would be a destruction. However, since this scenario indicates that there is a demonstrated safety problem, a solution must be reached that addresses safety. Perhaps the addition of superelevation, textured pavement, or warning signs would solve the problem.

Situation Number 2

Given the same scenario with the exception that the straightening is being proposed simply because current guidelines recommend a different alignment and that there are no demonstrated safety problems, a project-based strategy would be initiated. At issue in this situation is not that the road is historic, but that the project is unwarranted.

Situation Number 3

Our third situation involves U.S. Route 1 in Maryland, a historic route that has changed and evolved over the course of most of Maryland's history. The road has been widened, rerouted, rebuilt, and modified almost continually since it was first recognized. If the state DOT wanted to straighten a curve due to demonstrated safety problems, would this be a problem? Possibly not. Look at a project-based review. Does the road maintain any historic integrity? What is the context of the adjacent setting? Now? Historically? You may want to encourage a straightening that reflects the road width of the approaches to the curve rather than straightening the curve *and* widening the road, *and* adding shoulders, *and* clear-cutting the trees. The realignment of the road may not be an issue, but the manner in which it is done may, or may not, contribute to the character and context of the route.

LAKE SHORE DRIVE, CHICAGO, C. 1925.
Courtesy Chicago Park District.

Chapter 6
SAVE YOUR HISTORIC ROAD

Now that you've learned some basic concepts regarding historic roads, have had an introduction to the AASHTO Green Book, and have answered some detailed questions, it is time to determine the tools and strategies needed to save your historic roads. From community action to legal action, many options are available—bake sales and road rallies, minor policy changes and court battles. Consider the following ideas with the needs and realities of your historic road in mind. Remember, the simplest and most direct solutions are usually best.

∾ Research

LOOK FOR ALTERNATIVE SOLUTIONS

Investigate similar roads around the country that have used alternate standards or applied for design exceptions. Look carefully through the Green Book to determine appropriate guidelines or flexibilities that will enhance the safety of your road while recognizing and respecting its historic character.

DOCUMENT THE HISTORY OF THE ROAD

Build a strong case documenting the history of your road. Historic newspaper or journal articles proclaiming the technological advances of the road; documented associations of famous engineers, landscape architects, or planners; and historic photographs showing ribbon cuttings and first drives on the road will provide you with sufficient resources to prove, categorically, that it is a historic road.

ROBERT HURST AND DAN MARRIOTT INVESTIGATE A 1920S BRICK-PAVED SECTION
OF THE LINCOLN HIGHWAY NEAR ELKHORN, NEBRASKA.
Nebraska State Historical Society.

Community Action

THE PLANNING PROCESS

Statewide and metropolitan planning strategies have been initiated
under ISTEA to ensure that transportation decisions are being made
in a comprehensive manner to benefit the community as a whole
while creating an efficient and multimodal transportation system.
This new dialogue solicits greater participation from all the various
transportation users in the community and provides a forum for innovative ideas and discussions.

Such planning meetings provide ideal forums in which preservationists can introduce the issues surrounding historic roads. Rather
than waiting for a specific threat or trying to address too many different resources, you can work through the planning process for the inclusion of historic preservation in statewide or regional policy.
Hopefully, as a result, addressing historic qualities will become business as usual in your community. Raising historic preservation concerns prior to planned work will give you a greater opportunity for
the successful preservation of your historic road. Too often the

· WOODLAND PLACE VIADUCT·
·BRONX RIVER PARKWAY RESERVATION·
· WHITE PLAINS NEW YORK·

THE WESTCHESTER COUNTY ARCHIVES CONTAIN MANY ORIGINAL WORKING
DRAWINGS AND ILLUSTRATIONS FOR THE BRONX RIVER PARKWAY. ILLUSTRATIONS,
SUCH AS THIS ONE FOR THE WOODLAND VIADUCT, ENABLE HISTORIC ROADS
ADVOCATES TO BETTER UNDERSTAND ORIGINAL DESIGN AND FEATURES.
Courtesy of the Westchester (N.Y.) County Archives.

preservation community becomes aware of the potential destructions to a historic road long after the decision and the arguments in favor of such a decision have been made. This places the preservation community in the awkward position of trying to alter a project after plans, funding, and scheduling have already been determined.

The planning process sets up policy parameters by which, in theory, transportation decisions should be made in the future. The successful inclusion of historic preservation objectives in this process not only raises the issue of historic preservation to the state or region as a whole, but it also provides a policy decision to return to in the future if preservation is not being adequately addressed. It gives you the grounds to say, "This metropolitan area has a specific policy calling for the inventory of historic resources before plans are finalized. This project has violated procedure."

By getting to the planning table early, you will be able to influence decisions well into the future, you will raise the issue of preservation at a higher level, and you will reduce your chances of *annoying* the management entity with a last-minute request to acknowledge preservation.

MEDIA

The media (print, radio, and television) can significantly influence public opinion. Work to develop a strong relationship with the media in your community—this will enable your organization to publicly champion the cause of the historic road. Remember, reporters and media officials are not experts on historic roads. Your job is to educate them about the issues. Invite local reporters for a slide show or a drive along the historic route. Offer them an angle for their stories—"my grandfather helped to construct this road in 1895," or "did you know this is the only stone arch bridge of its type in the state," or "preservation rather than reconstruction will save the taxpayers X number of dollars."

If you are fortunate enough to have the press approach you, do more than simply answer their questions. For example, an employee of the National Trust was approached by a reporter from the *New York Times* after the Bronx River Parkway was listed by the Trust as one of "America's Eleven Most Endangered Historic Places" in 1995. The reporter's question was simple: "What do you hope to gain from the listing?" Rather than answering the question, the employee responded, "Before I tell you, let me give you a brief history of the parkway as background."

The reporter, knowing little of the parkway's history, was fascinated. The result was a lengthy story in the *New York Times* that solidly supported the listing, with frequent references to the parkway's history.

This story also underscores the effectiveness of providing reporters with written histories, fact sheets, and photographs that can form the nucleus of a story. Again, demonstrate your enthusiasm and support it with facts.

Finally, be aware of the tight deadlines the media face. Have responses prepared in advance whenever possible, and always return

SIGNS, SUCH AS THIS ONE MARKING U.S. ROUTE 66 IN ALBUQUERQUE, ARE AN EFFECTIVE MEANS OF INCREASING COMMUNITY AWARENESS FOR A HISTORIC ROAD.
Paul Daniel Marriott.

calls within a few hours. For you, a prompt response may be the difference between public awareness and public ignorance.

EDUCATION

The more people in your community who understand the history of your historic road, the greater the chances for preservation. Organize an education campaign. From lectures in the schools to interpretive weekend drives along the road, take every opportunity to introduce community members to the distinctive qualities of your historic road. Heightened awareness will build a broader constituency that recognizes the importance of preservation.

Monticello A Role Model for Historic Roads?

What does Thomas Jefferson's Monticello have in common with a historic road? Absolutely nothing. But Monticello and hundreds of historic homes across the United States can offer a valuable model for the historic roads advocate. Think about it—when you visit Monticello today you are presented with an accurate portrayal of Jefferson's life in eighteenth-century Virginia. Or are you? On closer examination you will find that Monticello provides the same safety and emergency systems (fire, smoke, and security), albeit carefully and ingeniously disguised, that all modern public buildings are required to provide. These are not eighteenth-century features.

Many jurisdictions across the United States have special building codes for historic properties. These codes do not excuse historic properties from the public safety features required of other buildings, but they do recognize the importance of historic character by allowing special flexibilities and alternatives.

DESPITE APPEARANCES, THOMAS JEFFERSON'S MONTICELLO POSSESSES MANY
TWENTIETH-CENTURY SAFETY FEATURES.
Paul Daniel Marriott.

Historic roads represent a new area of preservation. The means and methodologies by which to manage them are still being developed, discussed, and debated. Historic houses, on the other hand, are a well-known and appreciated historic resource type. When trying to convince others in your community of the value of your historic road, or when advocating flexibilities to standard design practices, you may find it helpful to use the analogy of historic houses in making your case. Don't try to exempt your historic road from modern safety considerations. Do try to achieve thoughtful and sensitive solutions that do not compromise the integrity of your historic road.

〰️

NATIONAL REGISTER LISTING

If your road meets applicable criteria and is not yet listed or determined eligible for listing in the National Register of Historic Places, get it listed or determined eligible. National Register listing is the principal form of historic recognition in the United States. Its established process represents the highest degree of credibility and legitimacy. While listing is not a guarantee of protection, it does carry with it certain federal reviews and (often) state reviews as well as considerable political weight. Contact your SHPO for information (see **Appendix C**).

The process of developing a National Register nomination will provide you with a comprehensive document addressing the road's history, engineering, and condition. It will prove an invaluable resource in the future that will help provide quick answers to questions that may arise regarding the historic road.

A National Register bulletin on evaluating and nominating historic roads to the National Register is planned for 1998. This bulletin will specifically address the issues surrounding the nomination of historic roads to the National Register.

You can contact the National Register at
  National Register of Historic Places
  National Register, History and Education
  National Park Service
  U.S. Department of the Interior
  Suite 250, PO Box 37127
  Washington, DC 20013-7127

〰️

HISTORIC AMERICAN ENGINEERING RECORD (HAER) DOCUMENTATION

HAER, a part of the National Park Service, interprets design and construction concepts and documents significant historic engineering resources across the country. Many roads and bridges across the country have already been recorded as part of a comprehensive long-range program. Your historic resources may warrant such study and documentation. In the unfortunate circumstance of losing a resource, HAER documentation prior to demolition will preserve for future generations the design, construction, and detailing of the resource through their documentary efforts.

To date HAER has documented park roads at Acadia, Yellowstone, Glacier, Yosemite, Mt. Rainier, Zion, Sequoia, and Great Smokey Mountains national parks; and the Colonial, Rock Creek and Potomac, and George Washington Memorial parkways and Skyline Drive. In addition to national park roads and parkways, HAER has documented the Merritt Parkway and the historic Columbia River Highway.

You can contact HAER at

> *Historic American Engineering Record*
> *National Park Service*
> *U.S. Department of the Interior*
> *PO Box 37127*
> *Washington, DC 20013-7127*

SPECIAL EVENTS

Special events, festivals, and drives can be an easy way of building a coalition and raising community awareness for your historic road. Antique car caravans, cleanup days, and picnics can link communities along longer routes for a greater sense of a shared history surrounding the road.

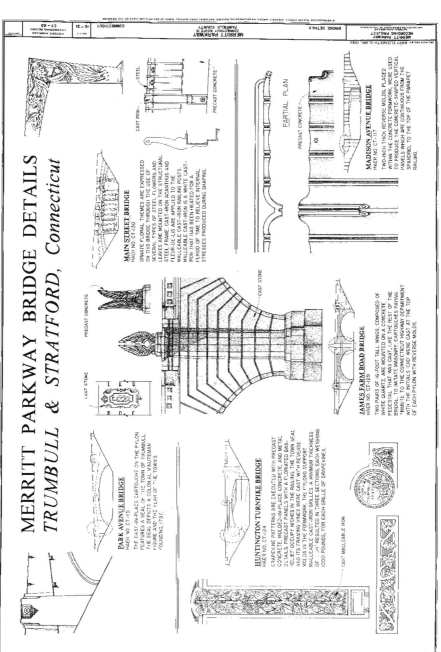

A Lincoln Highway sign–painting crew in Central City, Nebraska, c. 1915.
Merrick County Historical Society, Nebraska.

Coalitions

Find other organizations whose interests, while not focused on historic preservation, may be supportive of the preservation of your historic road. Many organizations with interests in environmental matters, economic development, aesthetics, or community growth may see the preservation of your historic road as a means of addressing or advancing their own organizational goals. An environmental group, for example, might see the addition of new travel lanes to your historic road as a threat to the air quality of the region. With other groups' assistance you can form a larger constituency addressing the preservation of your historic road.

Friends Groups
and Advocacy Groups

Organize a friends group or advocacy group for your historic road. Such a group can serve as a recognized entity advocating the preser-

EIGHTY YEARS LATER, THE LINCOLN HIGHWAY ASSOCIATION ORGANIZED
A WEEKEND PAINTING PROJECT TO RETURN THE ONCE FAMILIAR RED,
WHITE, AND BLUE BANDS TO THE ROUTE. PROJECTS SUCH AS THIS RAISE
COMMUNITY AWARENESS, INVOLVE RESIDENTS WITH A MINIMAL
COMMITMENT, AND, AS CAROL AHLGREN OF THE NEBRASKA STATE
HISTORICAL SOCIETY NOTED, "PROVIDE AN OPPORTUNITY TO INTIMATELY
KNOW EVERY SPLINTERED TELEPHONE POLE ACROSS THE STATE!"
Carol Ahlgren, Nebraska State Historical Society.

vation of the road. An official organization legitimizes your efforts,
and, if you officially register your group as a nonprofit organization,
you will be able to solicit funds and be eligible for grants.

RESIDENTS OF CHAGRIN FALLS, OHIO, AND CHAGRIN FALLS PRESERVATION, WERE
CONCERNED ABOUT THE DETERIORATION OF FALLS ROAD, AN 18-FT WIDE, 1924
BRICK PAVED ROAD. THEY WERE ALSO CONCERNED ABOUT THE PRESERVATION OF
THIS COMMUNITY RESOURCE SINCE NEEDED IMPROVEMENTS COULD CARRY
REQUIREMENTS TO BRING IT UP TO STATE STANDARDS. WORKING WITH THE
CHAGRIN FALLS VILLAGE COUNCIL AND THE OHIO DOT, THE RESIDENTS WERE
ABLE TO REACH AN AGREEMENT TO USE THE FLEXIBILITIES IN THE AASHTO
GREEN BOOK TO REPAIR THE ROAD AT ITS CURRENT WIDTH.
Henry P. "Bud" Evans.

George Washington Slept Here

Winding its way through the rolling piedmont and leafy foothills of the Shenandoah
Mountains, the Snickersville Turnpike has seen much history and little change in the
over 200 years since George Washington was a regular guest at a local inn. Today a
designated Virginia Byway, a drive along the road takes the traveler past productive
fields and eighteenth-century homes, over rushing streams, and between stone walls—
all along an alignment little changed since the Iroquois Nation established this direct
route to the mountains centuries ago. You can even travel the same curve where, during
the Civil War, Confederate forces, taking advantage of the road's alignment, surprised
and decimated the First Massachusetts Calvary in the Battle of Aldie.

Located in a relatively sparsely populated corner of Loudoun County, the Snickersville Turnpike has seen little traffic and consequently little maintenance—the road
was not paved until 1952. As a result of deteriorating road quality, local citizens peti-
tioned VDOT for some basic repairs. Of particular concern was a one-lane bridge located along a curve in the road. The citizens requested, with the support of the local
county government, a two-lane bridge of minimal width that would maintain the views

THE SNICKERSVILLE TURNPIKE IN RURAL LOUDOUN COUNTY, VIRGINIA,
HAS CHANGED LITTLE IN THE LAST TWO HUNDRED YEARS.
Paul Daniel Marriott.

to the water and the preservation of the trees that shaded the stream valley. VDOT responded with a box culvert—essentially burying the stream in a concrete channel, 25 feet of pavement with additional gravel shoulders, and the clear-cutting of trees for nearly 100 feet, all for a road with an average of only 1,000 trips a day.

Surprised, shocked, and angered by this interstate landscape, local citizens formed the Snickersville Turnpike Association to preserve the remaining character of the 14-mile historic route. The group, again with the support of the county, now advocates a 19-foot pavement width with grass shoulders and the use of wooden guardrails. When VDOT stated that wooden guardrail did not meet standards, the Snickersville Turnpike Association produced documents verifying federally approved wooden barriers.

The residents along the Snickersville Turnpike support enhancing the safety of the road. They have learned that constructive dialogue and, if necessary, repeated challenges to the status quo are essential to securing the community's vision for this historic route. As a member of the association said, "We will do what it takes. We will lie down on the road. We will not quit!"

For further information contact
  The Snickersville Turnpike Association
  PO Box 808
  Middleburg, VA 22117

∾ *Administrative Action*

SELECTION OF
SENSITIVE ALTERNATIVE DETAILS

If you have determined that the proposed changes are more threatening to the character of the road's details than its historic alignment, you will want to recommend and offer alternative design details that respect and maintain the integrity of the historic design. A road is a collection of details. The loss of historic lighting or stone walls may have a negative cumulative effect even if the road's alignment remains unaltered. Think of the countless historic light fixtures that have been replaced with galvanized steel cobra head fixtures. Or imagine your historic lights are being replaced because the wiring is bad and it is simply easier to drop in a replacement from the state stockpile than make basic repair. Compare the difference between a wooden guardrail and a steel one. How much aesthetic quality remains in a stone wall that has had a steel guardrail bolted to its face?

THIS NEW GUARDRAIL ON THE COLUMBIA RIVER HIGHWAY IN OREGON REPLICATES THE ORIGINAL GUARDRAIL DESIGN. SIGHTLY LARGER POSTS AND STEEL-BACKED RAILS ENABLE THIS NEW DESIGN TO MEET MODERN CRASH REQUIREMENTS. *Oregon Department of Transportation.*

Frequently such decisions come down to a lack of understanding or appreciation. The road manager is simply replacing an old lighting fixture with a new one. Both provide light. Both provide a barrier. What's the difference? Significant.

There are options available to maintain the quality and character of historic details. There are many good reproduction fixtures on the market. A few states have developed and tested guardrails and walls that combine historic appearance with modern safety. Many manufacturers offer reproduction light fixtures that meet modern breakaway requirements (a breakaway fixture is one that separates or breaks away from its base if struck, preventing the hazard of a rigid fixed obstacle). See **Appendix B** for a listing of alternative barrier details.

Pursue different safety solutions, such as a stabilized grass shoulder rather than an asphalt one. Rumble strips or textured pavement may heighten driver awareness when approaching a difficult area. The Denver Parkways have randomly placed traffic signals (not at intersections) simply to slow the traffic, which has a tendency to speed along the wide, straight boulevards.

If you are going to be modifying any existing details or adding any new details—new safety barriers, for example—be true to the integrity and original design details of your historic road. It would be inappropriate, for example, to use the stone-faced masonry guardrail listed in **Appendix B** on a historic route where the original barriers were a low-cost post and cable system (a 1930s barrier consisting of wood or steel posts with cable stretched between). Since the original post and cable system represented a relatively transparent barrier, an appropriate solution would be a modern post and cable system or a box beam barrier—both less visually massive than a stone wall. As aesthetically appealing as you may find the stone barrier, it would be an inappropriate and historically inaccurate installation.

DEVELOPMENT OF SPECIAL MAINTENANCE PROGRAMS OR PRACTICES

The development of special standards or maintenance programs provides an excellent method by which to manage a historic road sensitively. Such standards can provide the management entity with clear direction for the care of the unique features along the historic road.

Workers spraying the elm trees on Chicago's Franklin Boulevard
for elm scale in 1906.
Courtesy Chicago Park District, Special Collections.

Special direction for historic materials such as cobble, brick, or stone;
the maintenance of a historic landscape, or policies for repaving or
painting can all be addressed.

Development of
Alternate Roadway Standards

It is possible, under ISTEA, to develop alternate design standards.
Such standards may be used in conjunction with the Green Book on
NHS roads, or independently on non–NHS roads. In Vermont, for example, whenever the state design standards make a specific recommendation or policy it takes precedent over the Green Book on non-
NHS roads. Prince George's County, Maryland, has developed special
county design standards for historic roads under county ownership
and management.

Development of a
Corridor Management Plan

Corridor management plans (CMPs) represent a holistic way in
which to protect and preserve a historic road. A CMP presents a

comprehensive plan for use, management, and design. CMPs address historic features, analyze existing conditions, and present a method by which a vision, goals, and objectives may be achieved. Just as incremental destruction should be of concern to those wishing to protect historic roads, so too should incremental planning. In order to best preserve a historic road, it is wisest to have a game plan. Randomly arguing to preserve curve A, tree canopy B, or historic lights X, Y, and Z as a result of immediate threats positions your group as a difficult thorn in the side, always against any action. A CMP clearly places an overall expectation for the route and its preservation on the table. Thus, you can argue the preservation of an entire route, even elements that are not currently threatened, in an orderly and thoughtful manner. A good CMP will also give you greater credibility due to your comprehensive inventory and recommendations.

A CMP for a historic road would likely include sections addressing

- The history of the road (why preservation is important)
- The threats the road faces (traffic, maintenance, safety)
- A plan for preservation (addressing safety as well as historic details)
- Recommended actions (site-specific or corridor-wide solutions)
- Implementation plan (time, funding, and prioritization)

Ideally, a CMP would be developed by the road management entity in close cooperation with the local government, planning and land use officials, and local preservation organizations. Even if such an official CMP seems unlikely, it will still benefit you as a historic roads advocate to develop and promote such a plan for your organization's use.

SEEK DESIGNATION AS A NATIONAL SCENIC BYWAY OR ALL-AMERICAN ROAD

The National Scenic Byways Program of FHWA recognizes, through designation, routes of regional (National Scenic Byways) and national significance (All-American Roads). The program identifies six intrinsic qualities: scenic, *historic,* cultural, natural, recreational, and archaeological. A corridor management plan is required to be considered for inclusion in the program. Special funding and marketing assistance is available from FHWA for designated routes. The first routes were designated in 1996, including several historic roads: the Merritt Parkway in Connecticut as a National Scenic Byway; Trail Ridge Road in Colorado; the Selma-to-Montgomery March byway in Alabama; The Natchez Trace Parkway in Mississippi, Tennessee, and Alabama; and the Blue Ridge Parkway in North Carolina as All-American Roads.

FUNCTIONAL CLASSIFICATION

If your local road manager cannot determine your historic road's functional classification, you will want to determine the official designation. This will provide greater clarity as to what performance and safety expectations the management entity has for the road. In some instances, you may find that the functional classification is no longer appropriate to the road's use. You may want to advocate reclassification of the road to a functional classification that more appropriately defines its use.

DESIGN EXCEPTION

Design exceptions are documented approvals allowing a legal divergence from standard road design and management policies. For any road exhibiting unique resources or special characteristics, a design exception legitimizes the departure from standard practice, thereby reducing any claims of liability. Design exceptions apply to specific features—a single curve, a shoulder, a lane width. You cannot have a blanket exception for a historic road.

You should be aware that it is not essential to locate a solution for a historic road issue solely within the flexibilities of the Green Book. Design exceptions can and are generated for a variety of reasons to enable projects that do not fall within the range of values or expressed flexibilities within the Green Book. The design exceptions sanction actions and activities that are desired for unique road situations where a traditional application of the Green Book will not work. Design exceptions must adequately address safety and design issues and the reason for the exception must be well documented.

∼ *Legal Action*

Litigation should always be your last resort. Protracted court battles are costly and lengthy and can pit neighbor against neighbor over a resource you wish to preserve and protect and wish others to value and appreciate. However, it is always best to be prepared should litigation be the only available option. As a lawyer at the National Trust said, "Don't wait for the bulldozers to solicit legal assistance."

SEEK LEGAL COUNSEL

Legal advice can be valuable. Seek the assistance of a lawyer early, preferably a lawyer with experience in preservation, to give you guidance. A good lawyer can keep you out of a court battle and provide you with the necessary legal advice to channel your energies and resources wisely.

CONTACT THE STATE HISTORIC PRESERVATION OFFICER

As mentioned in Chapter 3, every state has an SHPO. Contact this individual early in the process. He or she should be able to inform you of similar legal situations within your state, indicate your likelihood for a court success, and recommend other sources of assistance.

THE MYSTIC VALLEY PARKWAY, 1916, OF THE BOSTON METROPOLITAN PARK SYSTEM. *Courtesy Metropolitan District Commission Archives, Boston.*

Change the Law

Concerned with the pressures highway design standards were placing on Vermont's historic roads and bridges, the state studied the issues, liabilities, and needs of these resources and their contribution to Vermont's landscape. The result was Public Law 140—An Act Relating to the Rehabilitation or Replacement of State and Town Highway Bridges—hereafter referred to as PL 140.

The law states:

In choosing between the improvement of an existing highway and complete reconstruction, the agency shall weigh the following factors:

(9) *the impact on the historic, scenic and aesthetic values of the municipality, as interpreted by the municipality, in which the highway is located; and...*

(d) *It shall be the policy of the state in developing projects as defined in subsection (b) of this section for the resurfacing, restoration, rehabilitation and reconstruction of bridges and the approaches to bridges to favor their preservation within their existing footprints, in order to ensure compatibility with the Vermont setting and context and to reduce costs and environmental impacts. Moreover,*

(f) *It shall be the policy of the state, as defined in subsection (b) of this section, to favor the rehabiliation of existing bridges. (PL 140)*

A WARREN DECK TRUSS BRIDGE OVER WEST RIVER, CONSTRUCTED IN 1928, BETHEL, VERMONT.
Vermont Department of Archives, Agency of Transportation Collection.

The law further states that "in rehabilitating a historically significant bridge, the design of the rehabilitated bridge must retain the bridge's historic character, to the extent feasible." (PL 140)

≈

BE A WATCHDOG

The federal government, every state, and almost every community have formal processes for public notification prior to any construction, planning, or land use activities. Remain vigilant of such public notices and announcements. The law generally provides an opportunity for formal citizen comment. Participate in such forums to advocate the preservation of your historic road. Further, be sure the government agency has adhered to the proper notification process. You would be surprised how often government agencies overlook public participation and open meeting procedures.

As you now know, the use of federal and (often) state funds can require substantive or procedural review of impacts on or to historic resources. Additionally, major projects will often require the preparation of an EIS as discussed in Chapter 3. Again, be vigilant. Make sure such requirements are being fulfilled.

KEEP GOOD RECORDS

Maintain good records and save public announcements, newspaper articles, planning documents, contract requests, and minutes of public meetings regarding your historic road. Additionally, keep a record of dates and times of any telephone calls your organization has made and correspondence you have carried on regarding the preservation of your historic road. Such records may be invaluable at a later date.

ENLIST THE LEGAL EXPERTISE OF SYMPATHETIC ORGANIZATIONS

Solicit input and advice regarding legal matters from organizations that will be sympathetic to your historic road. Consider environmental groups which may have experience challenging road construction projects. Seek the assistance of recreation groups that may have successfully lobbied for developing hiking or biking resources. Such groups have likely been involved with such legal issues and can provide you with valuable experience and additional support.

Naturally, you don't want to overlook the assistance and support of historic preservation groups. In addition to local and state preservation organizations, you may wish to contact road advocacy groups such as the Lincoln Highway Association or the National Historic Route 66 Federation. Such groups may be able to give you expert advice regarding legal issues specific to a historic road. Locally based groups such as land trusts, chambers of commerce, and convention and visitors bureaus can be important constituencies with experience in legal matters.

INVESTIGATE LIABILITY

Investigate the history of the road's liability. Has it been an issue? Have courts consistently found the road to be unsafe? Have most liability claims been heard in court, or has the management agency or government settled out-of-court? Get the facts. Don't rely on generalizations or anecdotal information. Obtain comprehensive accident statistics showing specific locations. How do such statistics compare to statewide accident rates?

Design Immunity

Design immunity is a defense to a lawsuit that a public entity can use for alleged dangerous conditions of public property. Typical alleged dangerous conditions of public property include improper highway curve design, improper signing or striping, dangerous location of trees, or absence of guardrail. For example design immunity suggests that the presence of a certain type of roadway feature, say a median with trees, may not pose a liability concern if it has a documented history of functioning in a reasonably safe manner. Design immunity may further suggest that such a feature may be replicated elsewhere due to the satisfactory performance of the original. In other words, design immunity raises the possibility of recreating historic features, such as the trees in the median, if existing examples and similar circumstances (speed, volume) can be documented as non-safety issues. Such documentation could support the request for a design exception.

The defense can be statutory (e.g., Title 28 United States Code 5 2680 (a), California Government Code section 830.6) or judge-made law. There must be a causal relationship between design and accident, discretionary approval prior to construction, and substantial evidence suggesting the reasonableness of the design. Design immunity can be lost if there is a changed physical condition (typically higher traffic volumes) giving rise to additional risks beyond the contemplation of the approving authority.

See generally, Cunliffe et al., eds., Selected Studies in Highway Law, *Washington, DC: (Transportation Research Board, 1988), Vol. 4 pp. 1966-N17 ff., Kentworthy,* Transportation Safety Law Practice Manual, *Charlottesville, VA: (Michie, 1996), Vol. 1, pp. 2–7 Aff; 45 ALR 3d 885.*

〰

Consider Litigation

If all reasonable attempts at preservation have failed, and if you are still convinced that your historic road represents a legitimate resource worth fighting for, you may want to consider legal action to halt the threat to or destruction of the resource.

〰 *Political Action*

Endorsement of Political Officials

Frequently a well-connected politician can be your greatest resource. Local and state elected officials will almost always respond to a situation that has demonstrated constituent support. Make a point of including your elected officials on any mailing lists, keeping them informed of meetings, and inviting them to events. Even if they don't respond or attend, you will have raised the awareness of their office—an invaluable contact in the event of a crisis.

A Resolution Acknowledging the Historic Resource

Seek a local or state resolution regarding the special qualities of your historic road. Such resolutions are especially valuable prior to any conflict. A generously written statement affirming the unique history of the community and special role of the historic road is nonoffensive and as politically palpable as mom and apple pie. Consider this example

Memorial Parkway represents a historic resource unique to our community. Designed and developed between 1920 and 1926, the parkway showcases the engineering advances of the early twentieth century in an alignment sensitively located in the Green River Valley. The parkway has provided generations of local residents with relaxing drives, recreation opportunities along the parkway corridor, and watershed protection. On this 75th Anniversary of its dedication we acknowledge this special resource and its contribution to our community's quality of life.

Statements like this can prove to be a valuable tool for you should a later decision be made that would compromise the quality of the historic alignment—widening the road, for example. After all, "you [local official] said it was important. Now you want to do what?"

RESIDENTS ALONG THE OHIO RIVER SCENIC ROUTE IN SOUTHERN INDIANA SECURED THE AGREEMENT OF 13 COUNTIES REGARDING THE MANAGEMENT OF A HISTORIC ROUTE WITH A BROADLY WRITTEN VISION STATEMENT: "THE OHIO RIVER SCENIC ROUTE PROGRAM INCLUDES PRESERVATION AND PROMOTION OF RESOURCES ALONG THE DESIGNATED ROUTE, AND PROVIDES MANAGEMENT OF THE ROUTE BY LOCAL JURISDICTIONS FOR SHORT TERM ECONOMIC DEVELOPMENT AND LONG TERM RESOURCE PROTECTION." (OHIO RIVER SCENIC ROUTE CORRIDOR MANAGEMENT PLAN, 1996).
Paul Daniel Marriott.

Keep mind that your key to success lies in your organization and credibility. Preservation is extremely important, but there are many means to a preservation end. In situations where the context and integrity of a historic road may be low, arguing pure preservation may not be as effective as arguing alternate solutions, mitigation, or cost. Understand the forces behind those proposing negative changes, and know clearly all your sources of support.

THE MERRITT PARKWAY, CONNECTICUT.
Jet Lowe, Historic American Engineering Record, Library of Congress.

Chapter 7
CASE STUDIES

The case studies in this chapter demonstrate the diversity of issues affecting historic roads and the creative and innovative approaches a number of different states and agencies have taken in advancing their preservation. These summaries are the result of years of study, action, and (at times) setbacks. They do, however, clearly demonstrate that good things can happen, that historic roads can be maintained and preserved, and that committed partnerships and education efforts can significantly alter attitudes and policies toward historic road resources. Each one of these success stories has involved a careful effort to look beyond traditional preservation and understand the other forces at play impacting the preservation of historic roads.

Note: **Boldface text** in the case studies denotes concepts and strategies discussed in this book as they have been utilized on actual historic roads.

～ *California: The Arroyo Seco Parkway*

DIANE KANE, PH.D.

From the relatively narrow Figueroa tunnel you suddenly find yourself launched like a speedboat in a calm, spacious divided channel. Channel is the word, too, for it's in the arroyo, below the level of traffic-tormented streets.

No brazen pedestrians nor kids riding bikes with their arms folded! No cross streets with too-bold or too-timid drivers jutting their radiators into your path. And no wonder I made it from Elysian Park to Glenarm Street in Pasadena in 10 minutes without edging over a conservative 45 miles an hour...

Such was the euphoric description of an early traveler along the Arroyo Seco Parkway in Los Angeles. Dedicated on December 30, 1940, the parkway was the first of its kind in the West. The limited-access, depressed road connected Pasadena with downtown Los Angeles, 6.2 miles away. Conceived in the parkway tradition, its designers had drawn upon similar achievements in the East, Midwest, and Europe for inspiration. Nonetheless, the Arroyo Seco had a distinctively western flavor due to the geography, climate, and relative isolation of Southern California.

At the time, the parkway was considered a leisurely, scenic drive, featuring landscaped embankments lush with native chaparral. Its curving alignment traversed a chain of lovely small parks shaded by sycamores and eucalyptus and provided views of the snow-capped peaks of the San Gabriel Mountains. The prohibition of cross-traffic provided additional driving safety and convenience and marked the road as a thoroughly modern invention.

THE ARROYO SECO PARKWAY AND FLOOD CONTROL CHANNEL EAST OF THE FIGUEROA TUNNEL, LOS ANGELES. ELYSIAN PARK IS IN THE BACKGROUND OF THIS 1940 PHOTOGRAPH.
California Department of Transportation, Headquarters Photography Unit.

Alternately termed an "engineering marvel" and "the big ditch," the facility became the prototype of the Los Angeles freeway system. Not only did the parkway indicate how to design freeways, but it became an object lesson in how not to design them. For example, the parkway was originally planned for two travel lanes in each direction with a wide, continuous shoulder. When early traffic projections prompted a redesign, the emergency shoulder was converted to an additional travel lane. The lack of shoulders was somewhat alleviated when intermittent safety bays were added in 1949, but this solution has proven less than satisfactory for stranded motorists and citation-writing highway patrol officers alike.

THE ARROYO SECO PRIOR TO CONSTRUCTION, LOOKING UPSTREAM TOWARD PASADENA, 1936.
California Department of Transportation, Headquarters Photography Unit.

Other design deficiencies, such as cramped ramp geometrics and limited acceleration and deceleration lanes, can be attributed to the project's tight budget, the topography within the arroyo, and the controversy over eminent domain at the time of construction. All three historic conditions resulted in a constricted right-of-way, leading to a road with unusually tight curves. The parkway's design quirks necessitated the early elimination of trucks; it also required prudent driving speeds and exceptional motorist courtesy. Still, despite these problems, the road provided an efficient and scenic route between downtown Los Angeles and Pasadena.

As traffic in Los Angeles increased, the parkway began to assume the characteristics of contemporary freeways. Average daily traffic counts crept up to 267,000 from the initial 27,000 in 1940. Average speeds also increased. Originally designed for 45 mph, 60+ mph speeds became commonplace. Higher speeds meant less merge time. Harried commuters exhibited less courtesy and common sense than the road geometrics demanded, resulting in higher accident rates. The lack of shoulders limited highway patrol officers' ability to cite wayward motorists, while highway crews were forced to close sections of the road for routine maintenance or else hazard life and limb.

Aware of these changing conditions, Caltrans conducted numerous studies to reengineer the more serious design problems. All studies concluded that the limited right-of-way, the environmental con-

THE LACK OF ADEQUATE ENTRANCE RAMPS HAS PLAGUED THE PARKWAY FOR MANY YEARS BECAUSE ENTERING TRAFFIC CANNOT REACH SUFFICIENT SPEEDS TO MERGE SAFELY WITH PARKWAY TRAFFIC.
Diane Kane, Caltrans.

straints of working in a flood control channel, and the possibility of disturbing protected parkland made changes to the facility both prohibitively expensive and logistically infeasible. In addition, the Arroyo Seco Parkway was **determined eligible for the National Register of Historic Places** in 1983. Changes to the parkway would involve scrutiny by the State Office of Historic Preservation, evaluations of adverse effect under **Section 106** of the NHPA, and answering to the U.S. DOT's **Section 4(f)** provisions. These additional environmental hurdles effectively prevented any serious changes to the parkway, despite mounting evidence that the road was suffering under 1990s traffic conditions.

Fortunately, the environmental constraints that have prevented changing the parkway are now working to preserve and rehabilitate it. In 1992 Caltrans was approached by Assemblyman Richard Polanco (now State Senator), whose legislative district the facility traversed, asking for traffic and appearance improvements. After again ruling out all the usual engineering solutions, Caltrans and the Senator hit upon a novel approach to address the parkway's problems. Since the road could not be turned into an ersatz freeway, why not use its historic character as the key to rehabilitation? As the Senator's aide, Bill Mabie, explained, "This road is an antique. Just as you wouldn't sit in an antique rocker like you would a contemporary one, you can't drive on this road like a modern freeway." In redefining the problem as one of motorists not respecting the character of the road, the solution shifted to one of driver education and code enforcement.

This cost-effective strategy, however, needed some legislative help to be put into effect. As part of the state freeway system, the parkway could not legally have speed limits lower than 55 mph. Consequently, Senator Polanco introduced legislation creating a new category of state highway—historic parkways. Once enacted into law, A.B. 1247 enabled Caltrans to **reclassify** the road as a parkway instead of a freeway. This simple change in status allows for lower posted speeds. It also qualifies the parkway for state and federal historic preservation grants which will be used to rehabilitate the road. Along with selective safety and landscape improvements in keeping with the parkway's historic character, officials are considering a concerted program of **driver education** emphasizing the parkway's historic qualities. New signs that either replicate the original signs or indicate the parkway's historic status are also in the planning stages. To recreate the original intent of the road as a pleasure drive, and to help motorists distinguish it from the region's freeways, visual cues such as a refreshed landscape, historic reproduction guardrails, lighting standards, and bridges are being investigated.

A multiagency task force was formed in 1997 to prepare a **corridor management plan**. Headed by Senator Polanco and comprised of representatives from Caltrans; the cities of Los Angeles, South Pasadena, and Pasadena; historic preservation organizations; and businesses and citizens in the corridor, the task force is designing an overall program to improve, promote, and manage the corridor on a long-term basis. Using the historic Arroyo Seco Parkway as thematic glue, the corridor management plan will highlight the many historic, cultural, recreational, scenic, and economic opportunities adjacent to the Arroyo Seco. Initial funding for the corridor management plan, along with additional funds for minor highway improvements, will come from Caltrans. Long-term projects will be funded through a series of grants available under ISTEA's Scenic Byways Program, the National Park Service, California Environmental Enhancement grants, and other funding sources.

The concept of restoring the Arroyo Seco Parkway to its original use and character in order to resolve traffic congestion and other issues is unique and unprecedented. Although it could be a controversial approach, so far it has been well received by public agencies and commuters alike. Many of the primary users of the parkway—those who reside along its borders—are practicing preservationists. They inhabit a landscape dotted with some of the region's oldest and most desirable neighborhoods, many associated with the Craftsman Era (a design period in the late 1800s and early 1900s when the beauty of natural materials, simplicity, and regionalism was promoted). They are as fond of the parkway as they are concerned about enhancing its utility and appearance. By working together, all interested parties can preserve the Arroyo Seco Parkway's past and, in so doing, ensure its future.

> Diane Kane, Ph.D. is an architectural historian and the Heritage Resource Coordinator with the Los Angeles district office of Caltrans.
>
> For more information you may contact her at:
>
> Caltrans
> 120 South Spring Street
> Los Angeles, CA 90012

❧ *Rhode Island: The Bellevue Avenue Reconstruction Project*

RICHARD E. GREENWOOD, PH.D.

When the National Park Service designated the Bellevue Avenue Historic District as a National Historic Landmark (NHL) in 1976, it acknowledged that this grand avenue in the heart of Newport epitomized a major phase in the development of American Architecture, and in our social history as well. During Newport's long reign as the Queen of Resorts from the 1830s to the 1910s, Bellevue Avenue was the principal corridor serving the exclusive neighborhood where the robber barons and industrialists played and the Vanderbilts' dinner guests hunted for jewels in sandboxes with silver spades. It was also where the country's leading architects produced masterworks, like Richard Morris Hunt's Breakers and McKim, Mead and White's Rosecliff. Such edifices embodied the material wealth and cultural aspirations of the Gilded Age elite.

The northern end of Bellevue Avenue, which lies in a National Register district (listed 1973), the Kay Street–Catherine Street–Old Beach Road Historic District, boasts important monuments from earlier eras in the city's history, including the Redwood Library NHL (1748), Touro Cemetery (1677), one of the oldest Jewish cemeteries in the country, and the famous seventeenth-century stone tower in Touro Park.

The depth and breadth of these historic resources make Bellevue Avenue one of the nation's most significant historic roads, and so, when the Rhode Island Department of Transportation (RIDOT) announced plans to reconstruct the road in 1984, it prompted vigorous response from the preservation community.

By the early 1980s the concrete paving of Bellevue Avenue was 60 years old and showing its age. Extensive cracking and patching gave the road a mottled look and trap rock (a very large stone aggregate), exposed by years of wear, made the surface excessively slick when wet. The condition of Bellevue Avenue was such that preservationists and city residents, recognizing that repair was inevitable, had already begun considering the impacts of repair and reconstruction before RIDOT formally initiated the project with a public hearing in the fall of 1984. These early conversations among the residents of Bellevue Avenue, **their city and state representatives**, and the Rhode Island Historical Preservation Commission (RIHPC) led to the formation of a citizens group, the **Bellevue Avenue Project Advisory Group** (BAPAC), and laid the groundwork for constructive dialogue and cooperation.

As the highway project was entirely within National Register districts, **Section 106** of the National Historic Preservation Act required RIDOT to consult with the state historic preservation office. Early in this process, the RIHPC and the BAPAC emphasized the crucial, and at the time innovative, concept that Bellevue Avenue itself was a historic resource; the concrete paving, bluestone curbing, and brick, slate, and gravel sidewalks all contributing to the districts' special sense of time and place. Therefore it was argued, the project should seek to rehabilitate these structures where possible, or if sufficiently deteriorated, **replace them in kind.**

The consulting parties, which also included the Federal Highway Administration and the **Advisory Council on Historic Preservation**, endorsed this concept and in a **memorandum of Agreement** (MOA), ratified in 1988, stipulated **design guidelines** for the historic road.

In some cases, it was relatively simple to work out the design details for the reconstruction. For streetlights and signposts, **research** by the city of Newport identified appropriate prototypes that were used to create accurate reproductions.

Other issues, such as the replacement of the deteriorated road surface, were more problematic. Although the original 1924 contract and construction specifications survived, RIDOT engineers were initially doubtful that historic materials could be matched with modern materials. However, after several meetings of interested parties to compare different mixes of cement and stone aggregate (cement, water, and aggregate make concrete) with a sample of the historic

AFTER CAREFUL RESEARCH AND PLANNING, WORKERS INSTALL NEW CONCRETE, BASED ON 1920S SPECIFICATIONS, ALONG BELLEVUE AVENUE IN FRONT OF THE ELMS, DESIGNED BY ARCHITECT HORACE TRUMBAUER.
Courtesy Rhode Island Historical Preservation and Heritage Commission.

pavement, the RIDOT Materials Section succeeded in producing a concrete that would match the original.

Also contributing to the success of the project was the patience of the Bellevue Avenue merchants and residents, who endured the longer construction period because of the floating, brooming, hand-finishing, and curing that concrete requires.

The sidewalks and curbs were reconstructed using existing materials where possible, although some materials, such as bluestone curbing, which had weathered poorly, were replaced with a more resilient quarry-faced granite with the approval of the RIHPC and BAPAC. The sidewalks were redesigned to provide for handcapped access, with the new ramps constructed with historically appropriate materials.

RIDOT incorporated special provisions for the project including tree-protective devices and root-pruning to minimize impacts to the many specimen trees and shrubs that line the avenue. The project also provided new street trees in appropriate locations.

Through a concerted cooperative effort by preservationists, dedicated planning and consultation at the local, state, and federal levels, and creative engineering and design by RIDOT, its consultants and advisors, the result was an outstanding preservation success. What had begun amid concern and apprehension in 1984 resulted, seven years later, in a project of which all parties could be proud.

Richard E. Greenwood, Ph.D., is a Historic Preservation Planner.

For further information you may contact him at:

Rhode Island Historical Preservation and Heritage Commission
Old State House
150 Benefit Street
Providence, RI 02903

Vermont: Historic Roads and Bridges

BOB McCULLOUGH

Vermont's historic landscapes (and the back roads and bridges that link countryside with community) are resources of inestimable value and are clearly worth preserving. Quiet scenery, however, can sometimes veil conflicting public policy goals. The need to preserve ecological, aesthetic, historic, and community resources must be balanced

U.S. ROUTE 2, WATERBURY, VERMONT, C. 1928.
Vermont Department of Archives, Agency of Transportation Collection.

against the importance of safe and efficient transportation networks, and this balancing act has created a debate of enormous consequence throughout Vermont. Both sets of objectives are deserving, both are vital to the economic and spiritual well-being of the state, and both can pose vexing, solution-defying problems. To help bring opposing points of view to common ground, Vermont's Agency of Transportation has launched two major initiatives that will have a direct effect on the state's ability to preserve historic roads and bridges.

VERMONT STATE HIGHWAY STANDARDS

A long-range transportation plan is now under way. As part of that plan, Vermont adopted **special highway standards** suitable for the state's unique landscapes. *The Vermont State Standards for the Design of Transportation Construction, Reconstruction and Rehabilitation on Freeways, Roads, and Streets* was released in May 1997. A Design Standards Committee, with representatives from planning, engineering, architecture, landscape architecture, and historic preservation, was established to evaluate highway design. That committee adopted a policy statement that defines good highway design to be "...safe and efficient function appropriately placed within the Vermont context." The statement continues:

CONCRETE ARCH BRIDGE OVER SAXTONS RIVER, WESTMINSTER, VERMONT, C.1926. (REPLACED 1987).
Vermont Department of Archives, Agency of Transportation Collection.

Highway facilities as part of the built environment should be designed to complement the natural environment and Vermont's past and contribute to Vermont's "sense of place."

As a general rule, highway and other transportation improvements should avoid negative impacts on natural, historical, and cultural resources and recognize that investment of these resources is critical to Vermont's continued growth and prosperity. When considering negative social and environmental impacts, the following hierarchy of actions apply: avoid, minimize, and mitigate.

Such forward-looking policy is a critical first step in achieving consensus on difficult issues. Accommodation of cars, pedestrians, bicycles, and trucks along a single transportation corridor is no mean feat, and the question of safety is one upon which reasonable people can differ. The Vermont state standards define appropriate highway standards with sufficient flexibility to encourage creative solutions for complex problems. Early and sustained **public involvement** was a critical part of the project design, and this, too, is a fundamental tenet in the committee's policy. Adequate **education** and effective communication with the public was equally essential.

A Parker Through Truss Bridge carrying Vermont Route 100 over the
West River, Jamaica, Vermont, 1929.
Vermont Department of Archives, Agency of Transportation Collection.

HISTORIC TRUSS BRIDGE STUDY

A second initiative involves Vermont's rapidly disappearing collection of iron and steel truss bridges representing the method of
bridge engineering that followed the state's timber bridges. Most of
Vermont's truss bridges are structurally and geometrically inade-
quate for today's traffic, and opportunities for preserving them grow
increasingly rare. The fundamental beginning point in any preservation effort should be a thorough evaluation of preservation alternatives, feasible and prudent alternatives to be legally precise, and it is
important to encourage local efforts—where the will to preserve
exists—to see alternatives.

Toward that end, Vermont has engaged an engineering firm **with
historic preservation experience**, most notably with experience
in historic bridges, to inspect each bridge to determine both structural capacity and traffic needs (present as well as future) that each
bridge is expected to serve. With that information in hand, the firm

will issue a report for each bridge and make recommendations from five preservation alternatives. In order of priority, these are

1. Rehabilitation/restoration for limited use on highways
2. Rehabilitation/reinforcement for highway use without regard to weight restriction
3. Rehabilitation and adaptive use to alternative transportation programs such as bike paths
4. Relocation and use under any of the first three categories
5. Stockpiling for future use under any of the first three categories.

Individual reports will then be assembled into a comprehensive whole to give a clear picture about the relative prospects for preserving each bridge. The firm is also being asked to develop guidelines for determining when the costs for rehabilitation become imprudent —at best a difficult analysis, made even more complex if one tries to quantify the value of historic resources.

The study is particularly significant because it allows an independent, highly qualified engineering firm to provide unbiased, factual information about the feasibility of preservation alternatives. This data can then be weighed in an objective fashion by two state agencies whose missions more than occasionally compete (the Division for Historic Preservation and the Agency of Transportation). If the study proceeds according to plan, Vermont will be able to reach consensus on specific projects with a clear understanding about the context of preservation alternatives for all the state's truss bridges. Equally important, this can happen without the delays and wrenching debate that have accompanied a great many past projects.

The Agency of Transportation has already rehabilitated six truss bridges, and plans are under way to repair another six. Adaptive use on bike paths, however, may hold the greatest promise, and planning for a large number of trails is currently under way.

Formerly with the Vermont SHPO, Bob McCullough is a lawyer and historic preservationist with the Vermont Agency of Transportation.

For more information you may contact him at:

Vermont Agency of Transportation
133 State Street
Montpelier, VT 05633

◆ *Connecticut: Preserving the Merritt Parkway*

PETER S. SZABO

In the late 1980s, the Connecticut DOT (ConnDOT) began a study of options to improve transportation in southwestern Connecticut, the fastest growing, most congested area of the state. One option, among a broad range under consideration, was to widen the historic Merritt Parkway. The study became a rallying point for preservationists, and opposition to ConnDOT and its planning process mounted quickly.

In the fall of 1995, ConnDOT, along with the Connecticut Trust for Historic Preservation, received a National Honor Award from the National Trust for Historic Preservation for its efforts to preserve the character of the Merritt Parkway.

The change in ConnDOT's attitudes and activities concerning the parkway was substantial and relatively swift (some have called it extraordinary). This case study will describe how it happened, what the results were, and what lessons were learned that might be of use to others concerned with preserving historic roads.

THE NEWLY COMPLETED GUINEA ROAD BRIDGE, SHORTLY BEFORE THE DEDICATION OF THE MERRITT PARKWAY IN 1938.
Connecticut Department of Transportation.

CONNECTICUT ROUTE 8 DRAMATICALLY CHANGED A SEGMENT OF THE MERRITT
PARKWAY WHEN CONSTRUCTED IN 1983. THE REBUILT SECTION OF THE PARKWAY
WAS STRAIGHTENED, WIDENED, AND PROVIDED WITH AN AMPLE CLEAR ZONE.
THE PROJECT WAS A WAKE-UP CALL FOR THE PARKWAY'S PRESERVATION.
Connecticut Department of Transportation.

Three factors helped make the effort to preserve the Merritt Parkway productive: it had committed leadership, it occurred on fertile
ground, and it employed an effective working mechanism.

In 1990, Connecticut voters elected Lowell P. Weicker, Jr., as their
governor. In turn, Governor Weicker appointed Emil H. Frankel as
Commissioner of ConnDOT. Early in his administration, Governor
Weicker stated his commitment to preserving the special character of
the Merritt Parkway and stated that a widening of the roadway
would not occur on his watch. Commissioner Frankel was also committed to preserving the character of the parkway, and he personally
led the core preservation effort.

Despite the relatively dense residential and commercial development of the 37-mile corridor through which it passes, the Merritt
Parkway retains a special character highlighted by its park-like landscape and 70 unique bridges. Many area residents believe strongly
that this character must be maintained. From this base of support for

the parkway, the **Connecticut Trust for Historic Preservation** rallied vocal opposition to any consideration of widening the roadway. On the strength of this movement, the Connecticut Trust was successful in its drive to list the Merritt Parkway in the **National Register of Historic Places in 1991**. Though widening was no longer an option, something still needed to be done to enhance safety and smooth driving conditions on the parkway. By the early 1990s, the 50-year-old parkway was carrying more than 50,000 vehicles a day, most at speeds in excess of 60 mph. The need for action, combined with the requirement of maintaining the parkway's character created fertile ground for the effort that followed.

The key mechanism of the ConnDOT-led part of the effort to maintain the parkway's character was the **Merritt Parkway Working Group**. The Working Group was a committee created in early 1992 by Commissioner Frankel to advise him on ways to preserve the unique character of the parkway that took into account its vital role in moving large numbers of people safely.

The Working Group involved individuals from inside and outside ConnDOT. Outside advisors came from the fields of preservation, architecture, and landscape architecture. Department representatives were drawn from the areas of construction, maintenance, design, landscape design, traffic engineering, property and facilities, and planning. In addition, the FHWA joined the group in 1993. Chaired by the Commissioner, the group met on a monthly basis for about two and a half years.

Through persistence, honest discussion, and **compromise**, the Working Group identified and hashed out difficult issues and created guidelines for treatment of the parkway in six key areas: design, landscape, bridges, facilities, traffic control devices/signs, and maintenance. In addition, the group suggested that **a landscape master plan** and a **bridge conservation plan** be developed to guide parkway management and restoration efforts. The Working Group process was interactive, and it led to mindset changes for all who participated. Those from outside ConnDOT came to appreciate the difficulty of managing this kind of facility, while those from within the department developed a greater appreciation of the roadway's unique character. These changes in perspective were perhaps the most significant achievement of the effort.

THE MERRITT PARKWAY TODAY. NOTE THE GUARDRAIL IN THE MEDIAN.
Jet Lowe, Historic American Engineering Record, Library of Congress.

The results to date have been significant. Historic documentation was compiled in the summer of 1992 by a team from the National Park Service's **Historic American Engineering Record (HAER)**. Nominated by the Working Group, the parkway was designated as a state Scenic Road in May 1993. In the summer of 1994, the Working Group completed a book of **guidelines and standards** for treatment of the parkway's many elements. Soon thereafter, a ConnDOT policy statement was issued affirming the special significance of the parkway and finding that all future work on the road conform to these guidelines. The landscape master plan for the entire length of the parkway was completed in the fall of 1994. Several projects recommended by the plan have been initiated. The bridge conservation plan was completed in late 1997. As part of the working group effort, a new, distinct signing scheme was developed with the goal of communicating to drivers that they are on a different type of roadway. Its implementation has begun. Plans were readied for a crash test of a new aesthetic guardrail made of wood rail and steel posts. Successful crash testing of this barrier was completed in early 1996. In the fall of 1996 the Merritt Parkway was designated as a National Scenic Byway by FHWA.

A number lessons were learned from this effort. First, success depends heavily on a demonstrated, firm commitment from top leadership in the form of rhetoric, presence, and resources. Second, the involvement of outside experts (e.g., landscape architects, architects, preservationists) will pay dividends. Third, financial resources are a vital element of any preservation initiative—they turn plans into action. Fourth, the future of historic roads is often inextricably linked to surrounding land uses; **engaging adjacent communities** is therefore necessary for long-term success. Finally, the Working Group process demonstrated that preservation and operational goals do not have to be mutually exclusive. Aesthetic requirements can be satisfied while safety concerns are met.

> Peter S. Szabo is the former Deputy Commissioner for Policy and Planning at the Connecticut Department of Transportation.

> For more information, contact:

> Maribeth Demma
> Director of Intermodal Policy and Planning
> Connecticut Department of Transportation
> 2800 Berlin Turnpike
> Newington, CT 06131

Nebraska: The Lincoln Highway

CAROL AHLGREN

The red, white, and blue signs that once denoted the Lincoln Highway are back on part of what is now U.S. Highway 30 in Merrick County.
—Morning World-Herald, Omaha

In 1913 a Lincoln Highway Association was formed to establish a unique memorial to Abraham Lincoln—a toll-free, paved transcontinental highway that would provide the most direct route from New York to San Francisco. An excerpt from the September 10, 1913, Lincoln Highway Proclamation states that, "the purpose of this Association is to immediately promote and procure the establishment of a continuous improved highway from the Atlantic to the Pacific, open to lawful traffic of all descriptions and without toll charges."

For the next 15 years the Lincoln Highway Association worked with representatives in the 12 states along the route to mark, im-

THE "SHORTEST AND MOST DIRECT ROUTE BETWEEN NEW YORK AND
SAN FRANCISCO." A POSTCARD OF THE LINCOLN HIGHWAY, C. 1940.
From the collection of Carol Ahlgren.

prove, and promote the highway. Despite political squabbling in the
East, deep mud in Iowa, and the deserts of Utah and Nevada, the
road did eventually catch on, becoming—as promoted—the first
transcontinental highway in the United States. By the late 1920s the
then familiar red, white, and blue bands marking the route had become a recognized symbol from Atlantic to Pacific. In 1928 the Lincoln Highway became part of the numbered federal highway system,
and the work of the original association was complete.

In 1992 a new Lincoln Highway Association was formed. Like its
predecessor, the organization was formed to promote the highway
and **increase public awareness** of the Lincoln Highway corridor.
In the more than 80 years since the highway was designated, it has
disappeared in some areas due to abandonment or new road construction. The new association seeks to rekindle interest in the historic highway and promote its preservation and interpretation.

In Nebraska the old Lincoln Highway is essentially U.S. Route 30,
with many early segments and routes intact. The Lincoln Highway
and its variants are located in the Platte River valley, a historic transportation corridor associated with the westward migration of the
United States. Paralleling the highway's route across the state is the

Union Pacific Railroad's main line (our first transcontinental railroad), portions of the Pony Express route, and the Mormon and Oregon Trails. Recognizing the history of the Lincoln Highway in Nebraska's transportation development and aware of the fortuitous position of the state in having so many original segments of the roadway, Nebraskans see the preservation of the Lincoln Highway as an important component in telling their story of migration and settlement.

Realizing that the ultimate preservation of the Lincoln Highway lies in **public education** and awareness, the Nebraska chapter of the Lincoln Highway Association has sponsored several events since 1994 to promote rediscovery of the highway. To celebrate National Historic Preservation Week in 1994, an auto caravan that included vintage automobiles crossed the state from Iowa to the Wyoming border (nearly 450 miles!). Selected older portions of the route were explored, and local residents along the route were encouraged to join in at any point and for any amount of time.

A highlight of the 1994 tour was a celebration at the Merrick County Courthouse in Central City. In 1913 Central City had gained the distinction of being the first city in the nation to endorse the Lincoln Highway Proclamation. These early "good roads boosters" posed

THE LINCOLN HIGHWAY CARAVAN PAUSES AT A ROUTE MARKER.
Robert Hurst.

LINCOLN HIGHWAY BOOSTERS ON THE STEPS OF THE MERRICK COUNTY COURT-
HOUSE, OCTOBER 8, 1913.
Merrick County Historic Society.

for a photograph on the front steps of the courthouse. In 1994 the historic photograph was on hand as the new highway boosters stopped for
a reception at the courthouse steps hosted by the Merrick County Historical Society and the Central City Chamber of Commerce.

In October of 1994, highway enthusiasts were invited to go for a
"Sunday drive" on the Lincoln Highway from Fremont to Omaha
(approximately 30 miles). The event represented a **partnership** with
the Nebraska Lincoln Highway Association chapter, the Dodge
County Historical Society, and Landmarks Inc., Omaha's preservation
organization. Over two dozen cars, including several vintage automobiles, made the tour. The highlight of the beautiful October afternoon was the 1-mile brick-paved section near Elkhorn. Participants
parked their cars and walked along the narrow road, which is listed in
the **National Register of Historic Places**.

A more ambitious caravan, from Omaha to Cheyenne, Wyoming,
was undertaken in June 1995 for the National Lincoln Highway Association conference. Joining the tour were participants from Illinois,
Indiana, Maryland, Pennsylvania, and Wisconsin. For most of these
out-of-state visitors, previous experience of Nebraska had been limited to a high-speed travel on nearby Interstate 80.

Some of the sites from the previous caravan were revisited and
several new segments of the route were explored. In some towns the

THE LINCOLN HIGHWAY TOUR, OCTOBER 1994, NEAR ELKHORN, NEBRASKA.
Carol Ahlgren, Nebraska State Historical Society.

caravan was led or followed by local residents. The highlight of the trip was Lincoln Highway Day in Clarks, a Merrick County town with a population of 370. Participants admired a newly completed mural of the highway **local high school students** had painted as part of a community improvement project through the Nebraska Department of Economic Development.

The caravan was enthusiastically welcomed, becoming a major event associated with the community improvement project. When the group arrived at the east edge of Clarks, they were greeted by numerous residents in vintage cars. The excited residents joined the caravan and, amid honking horns and music, formed a parade into town. The parade traveled through Clarks with crowds on both sides of the street. After speeches and a reception, the group was sent on their way west by area residents lining the Lincoln Highway and waving American flags.

Communities, newly aware of their Lincoln Highway heritage, have now approached the Lincoln Highway Association requesting assistance in preserving the road. As a result, an ambitious project is under way to repaint the historic red, white, and blue bands that the original Association developed to mark the route (see page 133).

Events such as caravans, local exhibits, and other activities can draw travelers to all sizes of communities and scenic rural areas along the route. A diversity of state and local groups, such as historical societies, chambers of commerce, tourism bureaus, old car clubs, and local businesses, can participate and benefit from such events.

Other benefits such as a sense of community pride and awareness of local history are less tangible than economic benefits but are equally important. Today, while older scenic and historic highways such as the Lincoln do not provide the shortest or fastest route between places, they can certainly provide travelers with a route that connects them to real places, history, and people.

As activities in Nebraska demonstrate, the Lincoln Highway has tremendous potential for community improvement, tourism, and local history activities. Given its proximity to the interstate, the Lincoln Highway is a great Nebraska resource, one that can provide travelers with a pleasant diversion for several miles or across the entire state. Local awareness of the Lincoln Highway has skyrocketed, creating a new, wider awareness for this significant highway and developing a new constituency championing its preservation and wise management. As one resident said, "We no longer live in a bypassed community; we live along the Lincoln Highway—the first transcontinental highway in America."

> Carol Ahlgren is an Architectural Historian with the Nebraska State Historical Society and the Nebraska Director of the Lincoln Highway Association.

> For more information, you may contact her at:

> Nebraska State Historical Society
> 1500 R Street, Box 82554
> Lincoln, NE 68501

Maine: Resurfacing and Rehabilitating Acadia National Park's Historic Motor Road System

H. ELIOT FOULDS

The 26.2-mile motor road system of Acadia National Park on the coast of Maine exposes the visitor to the full range of the park's outstanding scenery, from the summit of Cadillac Mountain to the rock-bound Atlantic coast. Begun in 1921 and completed in 1958, the construction of this system of automobile roads spanned a period of almost 40 years and is the result of a working collaboration among the National Park Service, the Bureau of Public Roads, and John D. Rockefeller, Jr. Rockefeller had a keen interest in the park because he was a nearby summer resident of Mount Desert Island. This interest led to his involvement in the creation of two separate road systems in Acadia—one for horse-drawn carriages and another for automobiles. Noted landscape gardener Beatrix Farrand designed many of the plantings adjacent to the carriage roads, and Frederick Law Olmsted, Jr., served as an advisor to the motor road system. Yet, in spite of the recognition given the Carriage Road System by the National Park Service, even by the late 1980s, there was little recognition of the historic significance of the motor road system.

National Register Eligibility

By 1989 the completion of a Historic Resource Study for Acadia's unique carriage road system was quickly leading to efforts to rehabilitate these roads which had been listed in the **National Register** 10

An Acadia National Park motor road showing "Rockefeller's teeth," as the guard walls are affectionately known.
Olmsted Center for Landscape Preservation, National Park Service.

years earlier. Research into the history of the carriage road system (1911–1940) had unavoidably overlapped with the construction history of the motor road system, and forgotten details of Rockefeller and Olmsted's involvement with the motor road system began to emerge.

During 1990, in celebration of the important work under way on Acadia's carriage roads, the Alliance for Historic Landscape Preservation held its annual meeting in Bar Harbor, Maine. During their visit, members of the Alliance took the opportunity to impress upon then Superintendent Robert W. Reynolds the significance of both the carriage and motor roads as complementary systems. The group made the appeal that the motor road system should enjoy the same level of recognition as the carriage roads through the National Register process.

In 1992 Superintendent Reynolds contacted the Olmsted Center for Landscape Preservation, based at the Olmsted National Historic Site, in Brookline, Massachusetts, requesting that the Olmsted Center conduct research into the history of the motor roads prior to the FHWA's completion of plans for the rehabilitation of a 6.77-mile portion of the system. The superintendent was concerned that earlier periodic maintenance projects had resulted in an accumulation of alterations which, taken together, threatened the integrity of the historic roads. For example, work on the Cadillac Mountain portion of the system undertaken in 1988 had introduced bituminous surfaces to roadside drainage waterways, in some cases covering historic rubble masonry ditch linings.

As a result of this request, research was undertaken that clearly revealed the motor road system's association with significant historic events, individuals, and the presence of high artistic value. An evaluation of eligibility was prepared for the National Register, and in March 1993 the system was **determined National Register eligible** by the Maine SHPO.

FHWA Project PRA–ACAD 4A10

Once determined eligible for listing in the National Register, Acadia's motor road system was conferred the same regulatory protection as a full listing. This included the requirement that the FHWA's plans and specifications for the proposed work comply with Section 106 of

BITUMINOUS PAVEMENT PLACED IN ROADSIDE DRAINAGE, CADILLAC MOUNTAIN
ROAD.
Olmsted Center for Landscape Preservation, National Park Service.

the NHPA of 1966. However, for this protection to be meaningful
and effective, additional detailed historical information was needed to
guide the FHWA as it prepared final construction documents for the
project. This additional research and the development of preservation
recommendations were undertaken during the summer of 1993 by
the Olmsted Center. The final report also served as the Section 106
compliance documentation for the proposed work.

The additional historic research revealed the piecemeal evolution
of the system and created an understanding of the **materials and
methods used in the original construction** of each segment of
the road. This new knowledge was used to develop detailed rehabilitation guidelines that addressed the treatment of roadside cross-sec-
tional features such as stone guardwall protection, waterway surfaces,
and masonry drainage features, as well as gates and signage. Historic

BASED ON SPECIFICATIONS DISCOVERED DURING HISTORICAL RESEARCH, THE STONE AGGREGATE SPECIFICATIONS OF THE CONTEMPORARY BITUMINOUS CONCRETE WERE ADJUSTED TO REFLECT THE COARSER PAVEMENT TEXTURE COMMON DURING THE HISTORIC PERIOD.
Olmsted Center for Landscape Preservation, National Park Service.

research even led to recommendations involving the nature of the bituminous pavement surface itself. Although this research effort began after the "plan-in-hand" inspection, when construction documents are typically 75% complete, **cooperation and compromise** between the park, FHWA, and the National Park Service's Denver Service Center allowed drawings and specifications to be efficiently revised, incorporating recommendations informed by historical research. Construction was begun during July 1994. **HAER documentation** in 1994-1995 added measured drawings, photographs, and research to the understanding of the outstanding engineering and landscape architecture of the park's carriage road and motor road systems.

One year later the project was completed ahead of schedule and at a savings of almost $80,000 below the original $1,395,279 figure, thanks to what FHWA project supervisor Greg Holnbeck refers to as the Dream Team of planning, design, and construction professionals of the two agencies. The success of the project was also assisted by the cooperative attitude and goodwill of the project's general contractors and subcontractors. According to Holnbeck, National Register eligibility and the requirement of Section 106 compliance added nothing to the final cost of the construction project because the added review created a situation where there were no surprises. In fact, taking a preservation approach in this project actually resulted in the deletion of some unnecessary aspects of the project and may have saved a modest amount of money.

Regarding the successful project, the FHWA supervisor stressed that, in road construction, the involvement of the preservation community needs to occur sooner rather than later in the project, adding, "It's a joy to do something for posterity."

H. Eliot Foulds is a Historical Landscape Architect at the Olmsted Center for Landscape Preservation.

For more information, you may contact him at:

Olmsted Center for Landscape Preservation
c/o Frederick Law Olmsted National Historic Site
99 Warren Street
Brookline, MA 02146

THE PULASKI SKYWAY, NEW JERSEY.
Kinney E. Clark, New Jersey Historic Preservation Office.

Appendix A
ROADS LISTED IN THE
NATIONAL REGISTER OF
HISTORIC PLACES

This appendix represents the most complete catalog, to date, of the historic roads that are listed in the National Register of Historic Places. This list does not include roads that are determined eligible for listing in the National Register.

The resource name, location in the National Register files, date of listing, and period of significance are included for each historic road listing. Most contain additional notes regarding the qualities or features that enabled the road to be listed. Individual sites and properties listed in the National Register are organized by counties. Multiple properties (definition following) are organized by state.

Roads that traverse more than one jurisdiction are not listed under every county through which they travel, but only under the county that comes first alphabetically. This is simply for reference and organizational structure—it is not to suggest that the road resource does not exist in other jurisdictions. For example, the Mount Vernon Highway listed in the National Register is located in Alexandria City as well as Arlington and Fairfax Counties, Virginia; it is listed under Alexandria.

MULTIPLE PROPERTY LISTINGS

There are instances when a historic resource may contain numerous components that are related—for example, a residential historic district, neighborhood park, and a railroad terminal. All were constructed at the same time and were part of a planned community. Each component is eligible for the National Register—yet individual listings may not convey the importance of the planned community as a whole. Therefore the National Register has a provision for the listing and recognition of multiple properties.

A Multiple Property Submission (MPS) establishes a Cover Context Document that explains the history of the properties and their relationship to one another. When you see an MPS listing you will know that the road resource is one of several road resources, or perhaps a road resource is paired with another component, such as a residential district, for example (nonroad resources within an MPS are not included in this book). Additionally, you will find references to Thematic Resources (TR) and Multiple Property

Areas (MPA); these references predate the MPS listings (established in 1991) and have since been replaced by MPS. MPS, MPA, and TR listings use only a state identifier for location—no county reference.

∼ *Arizona*

HISTORIC ROUTE 66 IN ARIZONA MPS

Arizona

Listed: May 19, 1989
Period of significance: 1926–1944
- Was the first national highway linking Chicago and Los Angeles
- Was associated with explosive growth of car tourism
- Represents the evolution of national auto transportation from dirt track to superhighway
- Was the main street through many towns
- Was abandoned for Interstate 40

Seven road-related listings are included in the Historic Route 66 in Arizona MPS:
Abandoned Route 66, Parks (1921)
Abandoned Route 66, Parks (1931)
Abandoned Route 66, Ash Fork Hill
Rural Route 66, Branigan Park
Rural Route 66, Parks
Rural Route 66, Pine Springs
Urban Route 66, Williams

∼ *Arkansas*

FACILITIES CONSTRUCTED BY THE CIVILIAN CONSERVATION CORPS (CCC) IN ARKANSAS MPS

Arkansas

Listed: May 28, 1992
Period of significance: c. 1935
One road-related listing is included in the Facilities Constructed by the CCC in Arkansas MPS:
Petite Jean State Park—Blue Hole Road District
- Constructed by the men of the 1781 Company of the Civilian Conservation Corps, Arkansas District, as a means of vehicular access to Blue Hole, a small swimming pond

- Constructed as a part of the overall plan to develop a public park to be administered by the state of Arkansas—now used as a Boy Scout trail

Dollarway Road

Jefferson County

Listed: May 17, 1974
Period of significance: c. 1913–1914

- Longest continuous stretch of concrete pavement in the nation at the time of construction
- First rural concrete highway built west of the Mississippi River
- First use in Arkansas of reinforced concrete in road and bridge construction
- First of many improved district roads to be built in Arkansas prior to the establishment of the State Highway System in 1923-1924
- Total length of 23.6 miles
- Known as Dollarway because the construction costs approximated one dollar per square yard of the road

California

Redwood Highway

Del Norte County

Listed: December 17, 1979
Period of significance: 1909–1923

- Highway through Redwood National Park and Del Norte Redwoods State Park
- Abandoned in the early 1930s for a new route inland
- Example of early state highway construction in California
- Highway established in 1909; construction began in 1917

Foote's Crossing Road

Sierra County

Listed: January 29, 1981
Period of significance: c. 1913

- Unpaved, built by A. D. Foote, a prominent western mining engineer
- Negotiates a precipitous descent into a canyon while maintaining a 7% grade
- 15.1 miles long
- Built to get gold from mines to Nevada City, California
- Hanging rock shelf still in use as an automotive road

Colorado

TRAIL RIDGE ROAD

Lariemer County

Listed: November 14, 1984
Period of significance: c. 1926–1941
- Built by S. A. Wallace, Roger Toll, et al.
- Engineering feat, the highest continuous highway in the United States
- Spectacular scenery
- 37.9 miles through Rocky Mountain National Park

RIM ROCK DRIVE HISTORIC DISTRICT

Mesa County

Listed: April 21, 1994
Period of significance: c. 1931–1950
- Linear district situated within Colorado National Monument, a 32-square-mile area of colorful and scenic geological formations administered by the National Park Service
- Paved, two-lane, two-way, 22.42-mile-long highway that runs through the Monument along the rims of the major canyons
- Rim Rock Road Historic District includes the road, three tunnels, and numerous associated roadway features which were a part of the road design including scenic overlooks, guard walls, retaining walls, culverts, ditches, drop inlets, and drainage tunnels
- One of the major purposes of the road was to allow travelers scenic vistas and views of the magnificent geological formation of the monument

DENVER PARK AND PARKWAY SYSTEM TR

Colorado

Listed: September 17, 1986
Period of significance: 1907–1914
12 road-related listings are included in the Denver Park and Parkway System TR:
East Seventeenth Avenue Parkway
Richthofen Place Parkway
West Forty-sixth Avenue Parkway
Monaco Street Parkway
South Marion Street Parkway
Williams Street Parkway
Clermont Street Parkway

Downing Street Parkway
East Fourth Avenue Parkway
East Seventh Avenue Parkway
Forest Street Parkway
East Sixth Avenue Parkway

Denver Mountain Parks MPS

Colorado

Listed: November 15, 1990
Period of significance: 1912–1941
Two road-related listings are in the Denver Mountain Parks MPS:
Bear Creek Canyon Scenic Mountain Drive (listed November 15, 1990)
Lariat Trail Scenic Mountain Drive (listed September 26, 1990)

❧ Connecticut

Merritt Parkway

Fairfield County

Listed: April 5, 1990
Period of significance: 1934–1942
- George L. Dunkelberger was architect of Art Deco bridges
- Created as an outgrowth of City Beautiful Movement
- Quick and pleasant travel from New York to countryside
- Planned by A. Earl Wood and Weld Thryer Chase
- Limited to noncommercial, recreational traffic
- Allowed no unsightly road developments and signs
- Followed formalized plan and regulations for parkways put forth by the National Park Service
- Began as a solution to traffic congestion on U.S. Route 1
- Named after Schuyler Merritt, the U.S. Congressman from Fairfield County who promoted the new road
- Landscape plan used only native materials

Route 146 Historic District

New Haven County

Listed: April 5, 1990
Period of significance: c. 1925–1935
- Road originally laid out in the eighteenth century to link Branford with Guilford

- Road upgraded in the early twentieth century as part of Connecticut's pre-World War II State Aid Road highway improvement program

~ *Delaware*

BRANDYWINE PARK AND KENTMERE PARKWAY

New Castle County

Listed: July 23, 1981
Period of significance: c. 1883
- Designed in consultation with Frederick Law Olmsted
- Originally designed for horse and carriage but now carries automobile traffic
- Provides vehicular corridor and a visual link between Wilmington's two major parks—Brandywine Creek and Rockford—while at the same time providing a quiet residential setting

~ *District of Columbia*

PARKWAYS OF THE NATIONAL CAPITAL REGION MPS

District of Columbia / Maryland

Listed: At different times, refer to each parkway for listing date
Period of significance: 1913–1965
Three road-related listings are included in the Parkways of the National Capital Region MPS
- Suitland Parkway (listed June 2, 1995)
- George Washington Memorial Parkway American Legion Bridge to Memorial Bridge (listed June 2, 1995)
- Baltimore-Washington Parkway (listed May 9, 1991)

~ *Florida*

VENETIAN CAUSEWAY

Dade County

Listed: July 13, 1989
Period of significance: c. 1926
- 2.5 miles long, links Miami Beach and Miami through a series of man-made islands
- 12 bridges containing 2 bascule spans connected by a 2-lane road

Florida State Road 1

Santa Rosa County

Listed: June 23, 1994
Period of significance: 1921–1944
- 6-mile section that was part of a planned "Old Spanish Trail" from Jacksonville to the Pacific Ocean
- Example of early brick construction technique
- First modern highway in Florida's panhandle

⟋ Illinois

Green Bay Road Historic District

Lake County

Listed: June 23, 1978
Period of significance: c. 1832–1925
- Green Bay Road established on a former Indian trail by Congress in 1832 as a post road
- Declared in 1925 by the state to be a pleasure driveway (based on a statute from 1889)

⟋ Iowa

Snake Alley

Des Moines County

Listed: September 6, 1974
Period of significance: 1894
- Switchback road built on a steep grade to enable access between residential district and downtown Burlington
- modeled on vineyard roads in France

Lincoln Highway in Greene County MPS

Iowa

Listed: March 29, 1993
Period of significance: 1912–1928
- Created out of existing roads that, for the most part, connected with the main streets of towns and cities along the route
- Was intended to establish the most direct route from coast to coast

- Through Greene County, the Lincoln Highway traverses the main streets of three towns: Scranton, Grand Junction, and Jefferson
- Created by the Lincoln Highway Association

Six road-related listings are included in the Lincoln Highway in Greene County MPS:

Lincoln Highway—Buttrick's Creek to Grand Junction Segment

Lincoln Highway—Grand Junction Segment

Lincoln Highway—Little Beaver Creek Bridge

Lincoln Highway—Raccoon River Rural Segment

Lincoln Highway—West Beaver Creek Abandoned Segment

Lincoln Highway—West Greene County Rural Segment

Kentucky

PETERSON AVENUE HILL

Jefferson County

Listed: May 1, 1986

Period of significance: 1902

- One of the last brick streets (or carriageways) left in Louisville
- Showcases early road-building techniques and craftsmanship
- Historically, Peterson Avenue recognized as a way to test the ability of engines—a car dealer would say that his car could make it up the hill in high gear
- The fire department tested new fire engines on Peterson Avenue

Maine

BACK COVE

Cumberland County

Listed: October 16, 1989

Period of significance: 1895–1925

Background: Back Cove, part of the Portland Peninsula, had mudflats, and smelled, and there were concerns for safety and sanitation. Area residents, concerned that the mudflats of Back Cove presented safety and sanitation problems, wanted the area developed into a park with sidewalks, driveways, and esplanade.

- Esplanade lined with 100 linden trees

- Power lines buried in order to maintain the view
- Designed by Olmsted, Olmsted, and Eliot and Olmsted Brothers

∽ *Massachusetts*

BAY ROAD

Bristol County

Listed: May 5, 1972
Period of significance: 1600s to 1800s
- Originally a Native American trail, served as a direct route from Boston to Taunton, Swansea, and Mount Hope
- Much of the 36-mile course is altered, but a 2-mile section remains unimproved
- Also known as the Old Post Road and The King's Highway

∽ *Minnesota*

MINNESOTA MILITARY ROADS MPS

Minnesota

Listed: February 7, 1991
Period of significance: 1850–1875
Two road-related listings are included in the Minnesota Military Roads MPS:
Mendota to Wabasha Military Road
Point Douglas to Superior Military Road

∽ *Mississippi*

ROBINSON ROAD

Leake County

Listed: November 7, 1976
Period of significance: 1821–1950
- Road connecting Monroe County with the eastern portion of the state
- Surveyed by Raymond Robinson
- Became a toll road in 1930 (a failed venture designed to raise money for improvements) and is currently part of U.S. 82.

Missouri

St. Joseph MPS

Missouri

> Listed: January 20, 1995
> Period of significance: 1910–1943
> One road-related listing is included in the St. Joseph Park and Parkway
>   System MPS:
> St. Joseph Park and Parkway System
> • Outgrowth of City Beautiful Movement, the parkways were designed to
>   move automobiles between the parks and within the parks themselves
> • Charles Mulford Robinson, George Kessler, and George Burnap involved
>   with the planning and implementation of the park and parkway system

Montana

Going-to-the-Sun Road

Glacier County

> Listed: June 16, 1983
> Period of significance: 1921–1933
> • A transmountain highway linking Glacier National Park's west and east
>   sides
> • Designed with the intention of creating scenic drive

Glacier National Park MPS

Montana

> Listed: April 4, 1996
> Period of significance: 1910–1945
> Two road-related listings are included in the Glacier National Park MPS:
> Bowman Lake Road
> North Fork Road

Nebraska

Lincoln Highway, U.S. Route 30

Douglas County

> Listed: December 1, 1987
> Period of significance: 1920

- Remaining segment of the first transcontinental highway; segment retains original brick paving from 1920—4,580-foot section, 18 feet wide

New Jersey

RIVER ROAD HISTORIC DISTRICT

Somerset County

Listed: March 21, 1991
Period of significance: c. 1738–1940
- A former Native American trail that became the north-south corridor for Somerset County; also used by both the Americans and British during the Revolutionary War

OLD MINE ROAD HISTORIC DISTRICT

Sussex County

Listed: December 3, 1980
Period of significance: Late 1700s
- Formally a Native American trail, then developed into a frontier road, and eventually helped shape the economic and domestic environment of the county
- Also known as the Trade Path, the Path of the Great Valley, the King's Highway, the Queen's Highway, and the National Trail

New Mexico

ROUTE 66 THROUGH NEW MEXICO MPS

New Mexico

Listed: March 24, 1994
Period of significance: 1936–1956
Five road-related listings are included in the Route 66 Through New Mexico MPS:
Route 66 Rural Historic District, Laguna to McCartys
Locally maintained Route 66, Glenario to San Jon
State-maintained Route 66, Palamos to Montoya
Abandoned Route 66, Cuervo to NM 156
State-maintained Route 66, Manuelito to the Arizona border

New York

RIVERSIDE PARK AND DRIVE

New York County

Listed: February 19, 1980

Period of significance: begun 1874, 1934–37

- Original design by Frederick Law Olmsted and Calvert Vaux as a parkway/park
- In the 1930s park and drive transformed by Robert Moses
- Contains a portion of the Henry Hudson Parkway

OLMSTED PARKS AND PARKWAYS TR

New York

Listed: March 30, 1982

Period of significance: 1868–1920s

Two road-related listings are include in the Olmsted Parks and Parkways TR:

Cazenovia Park-South Park System (Buffalo)

- Designed by Frederick Law Olmsted
- Includes Heacock Place, McKinley Parkway, McClellan Circle, Red Jacket Parkway, Cazenovia Park, McKinley Circle, and South Park

Delaware Park-Front Park System (Buffalo)

- Designed by Frederick Law Olmsted
- Encompasses Delaware Park, Gates Circle, Chapin Parkway, Soldier's Place, Lincoln Parkway, Bidwell Parkway, Colonial Circle, Richmond Avenue, Ferry Circle, Symphony Circle, Porter Avenue, Columbus Park, and Front Park

SUSQUEHANNAH TURNPIKE

Greene County

Listed: April 16, 1973

Period of significance: 1804–1901

- Early toll road that was also part of the road system used by immigrants going west
- Nine original mile markers and three stone bridges remain
- Two of the bridges no longer in service; the third rebuilt with original stone facing covering the modern materials

EASTERN PARKWAY

Kings County

Listed: February 7, 1984
Period of significance: 1874–1899
- First of Frederick Law Olmsted's parkways to be completed (1874)
- Developed as a part of a planned community and has 1,000 trees (including 25 original elms) along the 3-mile route.

OCEAN PARKWAY

Kings County

Listed: February 7, 1984
Period of significance: 1876–1899
- Designed by Frederick Law Olmsted
- First designed parkway in United States

OLD ALBANY POST ROAD

Putnam County

Listed: July 11, 1982
Period of significance: 1600–1899
- Road laid out over original Native American trails
- Improved until 1806 when the Highland Turnpike bypassed it
- Maintains original eighteenth-century alignment and dimensions with several of the 1797 milestones remaining

BRONX RIVER PARKWAY

Westchester County

Listed: December 13, 1990
Period of significance: c. 1915–c. 1930
- First automobile parkway in the United States
- One of the first uses of separated-grade interchanges for automobiles
- One of the first uses of a median to separate traffic
- Significant example of landscape architecture
- From the era of transition between recreational driving and the growth of the suburbs (limited-access, tree-lined roads, rerouting of natural features for faster travel, and scenic views)
- An early effort at pollution control and land conservation (developed in part to clean up the Bronx River)

Storm King Highway

Orange County, Hudson Highlands MRA

Listed: November 23, 1982
Period of significance: 1916–1922
• Picturesque, winding, two-lane highway carved into the rock face of a mountain

∾ *North Dakota*

Blome, R.S., Granitoid Pavement in Grand Forks

Grand Forks County

Listed: November 5, 1991
Period of significance: c. 1910
• Made from a portland cement-based artificial stone (with granite, crushed stone, and sand), and is an attempt to find a paving material that was strong enough for the new auto traffic but that would still have traction for horses
• The roads still in use today; scored and pocked to resemble brick-cut granite blocks

∾ *Ohio*

S. Bridge, National Road, NHL

Guernsey County

Listed: October 15, 1966
Period of significance: c. 1918
• Only brick curb to be built along the national road; built for safety reasons because of the 26-degree curve
• Good example of brick road construction techniques
• Designated a National Historic Landmark (NHL) January 29, 1964

First Concrete Street in the U.S.

Logan County

Listed: February 25, 1974
Period of significance: c. 1893
• First use of the wet method of pouring concrete (as patented by George W. Bartholomew)
• Only minor repairs needed in 1956; otherwise unaltered as of 1974

SOLDIERS MEMORIAL PARKWAY AND McKINLEY MEMORIAL PARKWAY

Sandusky County

Listed: January 25, 1991
Period of significance: 1918–1920

- 0.33 miles planned and landscaped in a cruciform design as a memorial to the Sandusky County war dead
- Brick paving with sandstone curbs
- Memorializes the slain soldiers from the region during World War I, the Mexican Border War, the China Relief Mission, the Philippine Insurrection, and the War with Spain, as well as the assassination of President William McKinley
- 50-foot grassy medians, with buckeye trees representing the dead soldiers
- Typical of City Beautiful Movement civic projects

HESSLER COURT WOODEN PAVEMENT

Cuyahoga County

Listed: March 31, 1975
Period of significance: c. 1906

- Extremely rare surviving example of wooden pavement, 8.75 miles long

⌒ Oklahoma

ROUTE 66 AND ASSOCIATED HISTORIC RESOURCES IN OKLAHOMA MPS

Oklahoma

Listed: February 9, 1995
One road-related listing is included in the Route 66 and Associated Historic Resources in Oklahoma MPS:
Miami Original 9-foot Section of Route 66 Roadbed

⌒ Oregon

BARLOW ROAD

Clackamas County

Listed: April 13, 1992
Period of significance: 1845–1919

- An intact 30-mile portion of the original Oregon Trail
- Remained a toll road until 1919

Columbia River Highway Historic District

Multnomah County

Listed: December 12, 1983
Period of significance: 1913–1922
- Built at the dawn of the automobile age, a technical and civic achievement because of its successful mix of sensitivity to the magnificent Columbia River Gorge landscape and ambitious engineering
- "A poem in stone"
- Cliff-face road building
- Reverence for natural environment important in its design

Rocky Butte Scenic Drive Historic District

Multnomah County

Listed: September 17, 1991
Period of significance: c. 1934
- A scenic, meandering drive up a butte that includes a unique tunnel, a butte-top observation post, and many stone road features (such as gutters and walls)
- Retains a high level of integrity

Rhode Island

Smithfield Road Historic District

Providence County

Listed: February 18, 1987
Period of significance: Mid-1700s
- Smithfield road one of the least altered sections of the Great Road—a narrow, winding, stonewall-lined road

Great Road Historic District

Providence County

Listed: July 22, 1974
Period of significance: Mid-1700s
- Road used to connect a number of Quaker villages to the markets of Providence; built in 1683, currently a two-lane asphalt road

ᓚ South Carolina

ASHLEY RIVER ROAD

Charleston County

Listed: November 21, 1983
Period of significance: c. 1691 to present
- A documented road from the seventeenth century that follows much the same route as when it was constructed
- Important historically for its impact on local economics and society
- 11.5 miles long

ᓚ Tennessee

FOREST HILLS BOULEVARD HISTORIC DISTRICT

Knox County

Listed: April 14, 1992
Period of significance: 1928–1938
- A two-lane curvilinear street paved with distinctive tan-colored concrete, low, squared curbs, and no gutters
- Early example of early automobile suburban street design that incorporated the street into the landscape (City Beautiful Movement)

TALAHI IMPROVEMENTS

Knox County

Listed: September 18, 1979
Period of significance: c. 1929
- A planned suburban community built around the automobile, scenic views, and the Cherokee cultural influences
- Based on Frederick Law Olmsted's 1869 plan for Riverside, Illinois

SOUTH PARKWAY– HEISKELL FARM HISTORIC DISTRICT

Shelby County

Listed: February 11, 1983
Period of significance: 1910–1936

- Three-block segment of the Memphis Parkway System located in the residential Midtown area in Memphis, Tennessee
- Four-lane boulevard with a wide landscaped median containing mature trees and shrubs
- Designed by urban planner George E. Kessler

MEMPHIS PARK AND PARKWAY SYSTEM MPS

Tennessee

Listed: July 3, 1989

Period of significance: 1900–1939

One road-related listing is included in the Memphis Park and Parkway System MPS:

Memphis Parkway System

- Significant example of an intact urban parkway system designed to encourage residential growth and use of city parks
- Medians planted with trees and shrubs
- Only parkway system in Tennessee implemented during the City Beautiful Movement
- Designed by George Kessler, noted planner and landscape architect

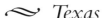 # *Texas*

MISSION PARKWAY

Bexar County

Listed: June 3, 1975

Period of significance: c. 1900

- A parkway based on residential and historical features. Four Spanish colonial Missions—Nuestra Senora Purisima Concepcion de Acuna, San Jose y San Miguel de Aguayo, San Juan Capistrano, and San Francisco de la Espada—unify the parkway

MOTHER NEFF STATE PARK AND F.A.S. 21-B (1) HISTORIC DISTRICT

Coryell County

Listed: September 2, 1992

Period of significance: c. 1920

- Designed in the 1920s as a scenic parkway
- Renovated by the Civilian Conservation Corps during the 1930s

KING'S HIGHWAY
HISTORIC DISTRICT

Dallas County, Oak Cliffs MPS

Listed: June 17, 1994

HEIGHTS BOULEVARD ESPLANADE

Harris County

Listed: May 9, 1983
Period of significance: c. 1892
- Boulevard a focus for the affluent housing of the area
- First paved road in the area

BROADWAY BLUFF IMPROVEMENTS

Nueces County

Listed: August 29, 1988
Period of significance: c. 1914
- Alexander Plotter designed a planned community based on the City Beautiful Movement
- Designed to improve the appearance of a bluff, used elements from the natural landscape and vertical division of the roads

U.S. ROUTE 66—
SIXTH STREET HISTORIC DISTRICT

Potter County

Listed: August 23, 1994

Utah

ZION NATIONAL PARK MRA

Utah

Listed: February 16, 1996
Period of significance: 1901–1940
One road-related listing is included in the Zion National Park MRA: Floor of the Valley Road
- A paved, two-lane scenic park road, located in Zion National Park in southwestern Utah; 9 miles long, flanked by towering sandstone cliffs

- Designed to harmonize with surrounding landscapes, uses a red tinted chip sealer on the roadbed itself and native sandstone blocks in the construction of associated features

ZION–MOUNT CARMEL HIGHWAY

Washington County

Listed: July 7, 1987
Period of significance: c. 1901–1940
- Significant due to design by Thomas H. MacDonald
- Road links Zion National Park, Bryce Canyon National Park, Cedar Breaks, and the north rim of the Grand Canyon
- Road noted for its scenic characteristics

Vermont

BROOKFIELD VILLAGE HISTORIC DISTRICT

Orange County

Listed: November 8, 1973
Period of significance: 1800s
- A picturesque unpaved (as of 1973) main street that follows the route of a historic road (the Montpeleir to Randolf Stage Road)

HISTORIC CROWN POINT ROAD

Windsor County

Listed: September 24, 1974
Period of significance: c. 1760
- A dirt road/trail that played a key role in the French and Indian War and the Revolutionary War
- A travel route for the settlers going from Massachusetts to New Hampshire
- Unimproved for automobile traffic

Virginia

SOUTHWEST MOUNTAIN RURAL HISTORIC DISTRICT

Albemarle County

Listed: February 27, 1992
Period of significance: 1760–1941

- Old Mountain Road—Route 22—still follows its original route and is a two-lane paved highway with few improvements; also included in the District is an unpaved portion of the Fredericksburg Road, also from the mid-eighteenth century
- Associated with Peter Jefferson, Thomas Jefferson, and Merriwether Lewis

MOUNT VERNON MEMORIAL HIGHWAY

Alexandria Independent City

Listed; May 18, 1981
Period of significance: c. 1929–1932

- Portion of the George Washington Memorial Parkway, paralleling the Potomac River, was designed and landscaped to maximize scenic, esthetic, and commemorative qualities
- Designed to provide drivers striking vistas of national monuments as well as scenery
- Links Washington, D.C. with Mount Vernon
- First highway constructed and maintained by the National Park Service

✍ *West Virginia*

HOPKINS MOUNTAIN HISTORIC DISTRICT

Greenbrier County

Listed: April 4, 1994
Period of significance: c. 1933

- Contains the Hopkins Mountain Road, which was originally a service road for the U.S. Forest Service, but was renovated into a two-lane road by the CCC in the 1930s

✍ *Washington*

THE YELLOWSTONE ROAD

King County

Listed: December 2, 1974
Period of significance: c. 1913

- Part of the Yellowstone Trail, one of the four major highways crossing the nation linking the Pacific to the Atlantic; northernmost route connecting Boston to Seattle via Cleveland, Chicago, Minneapolis, and others
- Paved in brick

GRANDVIEW ROAD–YELLOWSTONE TRAIL

Yakima County

Listed: December 11, 1995
Period of significance: c. 1909–1930

- 3-mile section of concrete roadway, an intact remnant of the historic Yellowstone Trail, one of four major transcontinental automobile highways established in United States during early twentieth century; use of concrete paving as an early example of engineering efforts to upgrade this important regional transportation corridor

Wisconsin

LAKE PARK

Milwaukee County

Listed: April 22, 1993
Period of significance: c. 1892

- Designed by Frederick Law Olmsted in 1892 for recreational driving
- First city-owned park in Milwaukee

DELAVAN'S VITRIFIED BRICK STREET

Walworth County

Listed: March 7, 1996
Period of significance: c. 1913

- Interesting use of vitrified brick (heavily fired bricks that are impervious to water and stronger than regular bricks); shows a transition period from the dirt street to modern asphalt and the attempts that were made to find a suitable paving material that could withstand the pressures of automobile traffic

HIGHLAND BOULEVARD DISTRICT

Milwaukee

Listed: July 30, 1985
Period of significance: 1895–1915

- Boulevard planned by the Milwaukee Common Council to create public thruways, prohibiting undesirable traffic and providing links to city parks
- A landscaped esplanade fronted by long blocks of monumental residences on broad lots with wide setbacks from the road

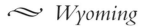
❧ *Wyoming*

Bridger Immigrant Road—Dry Creek Crossing

Big Horn County

Listed: January 7, 1975

Period of significance: 1800s and 1900s

- Built by Jim Bridger to provide a safer and easier way west
- Used by immigrants and miners going the Montana Gold Fields (it cut about a third of the travel time off of the Oregon trail route to the gold fields
- Now abandoned with only two sections remaining, including the nominated section of Dry Creek Crossing

Appendix B

APPROVED ALTERNATIVE GUARDRAIL, GUARDWALL, AND BRIDGE RAIL DESIGNS

∾ Steel-Backed Timber Guardrail

The steel-backed timber guardrail maintains the aesthetic qualities of traditional wood guardrail with a reinforcing steel component to meet modern crash tests. The steel-backed timber guardrail functions much like any post and beam system. The timber and steel rails prevent errant vehicles from penetrating the barrier line. The rail loads are then transmitted to the ground through the posts (as in traditional galvanized steel W-beam guardrail). The steel-backed timber guardrail can be constructed in blocked-out and unblocked-out versions. The blocked-out version has an additional

STEEL-BACKED TIMBER GUARDRAIL, BY KEY BRIDGE, ALONG THE GEORGE WASHING-
TON MEMORIAL PARKWAY, VIRGINIA. THIS VERSION, BLOCKED OUT, REDUCES SNAG-
GING IF STRUCK (THE BLOCK-OUT KEEPING THE FACE OF THE RAIL SEVERAL INCHES
IN FRONT OF THE POST.
Paul Daniel Marriott.

wood member between the rail and the post. This additional few inches helps prevent an errant vehicle from striking the guardrail post and makes it easier for the vehicle to return to the roadway. Blocking out is recommended for higher speeds.

Developed by
The National Park Service and The Federal Lands Highways Division of the FHWA

Tested and approved
FHWA Test 1818-5-6-87, October 26, 1987, blocked-out version
FHWA Test 1818-8-88, December 21, 1988, blocked-out version
FHWA Test 1818-14-88, July 20, 1988, unblocked-out version

Maximum speed for use
Federal Lands Highways Division of the FHWA approves the blocked-out version for all situations. The unblocked-out version is allowed for speeds of less than 50 mph (80 kph).

Recommended use
The steel-backed timber guardrail is recommended for historic parkways and highways where a natural or rustic solution is desirable.

In service
George Washington Memorial Parkway, Virginia
Baltimore Washington Parkway, Maryland
Natchez Trace Parkway, Tennessee
Great Smokey Mountains National Park, Tennessee
Blue Ridge Parkway, Virginia

For additional information
Report number FHWA-SA-91-051
Summary Report on Aesthetic Bridge Rails and Guardrails
U.S. Department of Transportation
Federal Highway Administration
June 1992

Concrete-Core Stone Masonry Guardwall

The stone masonry guardwall resembles the native stone walls that were installed on parkways and scenic roads in the early part of the twentieth century. These early walls, usually mortared or dry laid, do not perform well in modern crash tests. The concrete-core stone masonry guardwall has a reinforced concrete core with a stone facing (usually and preferably of native stone) capable of providing modern safety. The stone facia (stone veneer)

THE CONCRETE CORE BEING INSTALLED ALONG SKYLINE DRIVE IN VIRGINIA.
Paul Daniel Marriott.

NATIVE STONE LAID UP TO CONCEAL THE CONCRETE CENTER CORE.
Paul Daniel Marriott.

THE COMPLETED CONCRETE-CORE STONE GUARDWALL ON SKYLINE DRIVE.
Paul Daniel Marriott.

cannot project any more than 1.5 in. (38 millimeters [mm]) from a neat
line—an imaginary line representing the average face of an irregular surface.
This minor 1.5-in. variation in the stone ensures a relatively uniform surface
that is better able to deflect an errant vehicle should it strike the wall—
jagged and irregular surfaces can snag an automobile and make it more difficult for the driver to regain control.

While this guardwall is a significant improvement over a concrete jersey
barrier, some have criticized this wall for being monotonous and bland
when compared with the earlier more varied, occasionally highly irregular,
walls that are being replaced.

Developed by
The National Park Service and The Federal Lands Highway Division of
FHWA

Tested and approved
FHWA Test 1818-5-3-87, October 29, 1987
FHWA Test 1818-5-4-87, November 5, 1987
FHWA Test 1818-5-88, May 23, 1988

Maximum speed for use
Federal Lands Highways Division of the FHWA recommends the concrete-
core stone masonry guardwall for roads with a design speed of 60 mph (97
kph) or less.

Recommended use

This barrier is recommended for historic roads where stone walls were originally developed and in historic areas needing an aesthetic barrier where native stone is a recognized and appropriate building material.

In service

Skyline Drive, Shenandoah National Park, Virginia
Foothills Parkway, Great Smokey Mountains National Park, Tennessee
George Washington Memorial Parkway, Virginia

For additional information

Report number FHWA-SA-91-051
"Summary Report on Aesthetic Bridge Rails and Guardrails"
U.S. Department of Transportation
Federal Highway Administration
June 1992

∾ *Precast Simulated Stone Guardwall*

The precast simulated stone guardwall functions like any rigid concrete barrier (such as a jersey barrier) while providing enhanced aesthetics. The barrier is made of precast concrete panels designed, textured, and colored to resemble natural masonry. The pigments used to color the stone can be adjusted according to the natural stone color of the area. Additionally, the stone pattern can be adjusted to match existing stone work such as that

PRECAST SIMULATED STONE WALLS ALONG THE BALTIMORE WASHINGTON PARKWAY IN MARYLAND.
Paul Daniel Marriott.

found on walls and bridges. It is an effective alternative, especially where higher speeds make the simulated stone and repeating pattern barely perceptible to the passing motorist.

Developed by
The National Park Service and The Federal Lands Highways Division of FHWA

Tested and approved
FHWA Test 1818-7-88, December 1, 1988
FHWA Test 1818-12-88, September 29, 1988

Maximum speed for use
Federal Lands Highways Division has approved the precast simulated guardwall for roadways with design speeds of 60 mph (97 kph) or less.

Recommended use
The precast simulated stone guardwall is recommended for roads with higher speeds where pedestrian contact is at a minimum. The wall is attractive and looks authentic at higher speeds (the installed walls along the Baltimore Washington Parkway were believed to be stone by many trained professionals).

In service
The Baltimore Washington Parkway, Maryland

For additional information
Report number FHWA-SA-91-051
"Summary Report on Aesthetic Bridge Rails and Guardrails"
U.S. Department of Transportation
Federal Highway Administration
June 1992

ᕦ *Glue-Laminated Wood Bridge Rail*

Glue-laminated wood bridge rails provide the traditional aesthetic qualities of wood with a stronger and more durable alternative. This rail is intended for use on low-service level bridges. The design of the rail allows for views to be maintained. Like the steel-backed timber guardrail, this rail is recommended for use with a block-out.

Developed by
U.S. Forest Service

Tested and approved
WB-1, September 12, 1988
WB-2, September 27, 1988

Maximum speed for use
To be determined. Testing underway.

Recommended use
The glue-laminated wood bridge railing is recommended for lower speed roads. Its design enables it to blend well with the natural landscape.

In service
Installed in many national forests and on rural country roads that provide access to national forests.

For additional information
Report number FHWA-SA-91-051
"Summary Report on Aesthetic Bridge Rails and Guardrails"
U.S. Department of Transportation
Federal Highway Administration
June 1992

~ *Federal Lands Highways Modified Kansas Corral Bridge Railing*

The Federal Lands Highways modified Kansas corral bridge railing provides a more open and aesthetic solution to the standard jersey barrier generally used on bridges. Its post and beam construction is of reinforced concrete. The railing is 27 in. (688 mm) high.

Developed by
Federal Lands Highways Division of FHWA
Tested and approved
FHWA Test KM-1, November 18, 1988
FHWA Test KM-2, August 17, 1988

Maximum speed for use
To be determined. Testing underway.

Recommended use
Federal Lands Highways modified Kansas corral bridge railing is recommended for installations where an aesthetic yet contemporary design is sought.

In service
Olympic National Park
Grand Teton National Park

For additional information
Report number FHWA-SA-91-051
"Summary Report on Aesthetic Bridge Rails and Guardrails"

U.S. Department of Transportation
Federal Highway Administration
June 1992

∿ *Columbia River Gorge Guardrail*

Developed by the Oregon DOT for use on the historic Columbia River Gorge Highway, this guardrail replicates the post and beam system originally designed for the route and updates it with a reinforced steel-backed design that meets modern crash test requirements.

Developed by
Oregon Department of Transportation

Tested and approved
Texas Transportation Institute, 1990

Maximum speed for use
50 mph

Recommended use
Historic roads where a post and two rail guardrail was originally installed

In service
Columbia River Gorge Highway, Oregon

For additional information
Oregon DOT

THE COLUMBIA RIVER HIGHWAY GUARDRAIL. SLIGHTLY LARGER POSTS THAN THE ORIGINAL, AND STEEL-BACK BEAMS ALLOW THIS CLOSE LOOK ALIKE TO MEET ALL REQUIRED CRASH TESTS.
Michael J. O'Hara, Jr.

DETAIL OF COLUMBIA RIVER HIGHWAY GUARDRAIL.
Michael J. O'Hara, Jr.

∾ *Design Your Own*

There is always the possibility of designing a bridge rail, guardrail, or guard-wall incorporating enhanced safety features to meet the specific design and aesthetic concerns of your historic road. Once designed, you must develop a prototype that can be crash tested (cars are literally driven into the barrier) to ensure that its design will perform at acceptable levels.

Designing and developing your own barrier is generally the most time consuming and costly alternative. However it may be your only and best choice to maintain the historic character of your road. If you do determine that designing your own barrier is your best alternative, you may wish to consult with advocacy groups with similar historic roads or with states in which such barriers may be historically appropriate. You may be able to es-tablish a partnership for the design, development, testing, and funding of the new barrier. States are allowed to pool FHWA research funds (distributed to each state) for joint projects.

Appendix C

U.S. STATE, COMMONWEALTH, AND TERRITORIAL HISTORIC PRESERVATION OFFICES

State historic preservation offices are mandated by the U.S. Congress. These offices, in every state and territory, can make you aware of pertinent federal and state historic preservation policies and laws. Additionally, they will be able to put you in contact with any appropriate local or state preservation offices that may be able to assist you.

ALABAMA

Alabama Historical Commission
468 South Perry Street
Montgomery, AL 36130-3477
334-242-3184
334-240-3477, FAX

ALASKA

Alaska Department of Natural Resources
Office of History and Archaeology
Division of Parks
3601 "C" Street, Suite 1278
Anchorage, AK 99503-5921
907-269-8721
907-269-8908, FAX

ARIZONA

Arizona State Parks
1300 West Washington
Phoenix, AZ 85007
602-542-4174
602-542-4180, FAX

ARKANSAS

Arkansas Historic Preservation
    Program
323 Center Street, Suite 1500
Little Rock, AR 72201
501-324-9880
501-324-9184, FAX

CALIFORNIA

Office of Historic Preservation
Department of Parks and Recreation
PO Box 942896
Sacramento, CA 94296-0001
916-653-6624
916-653-9824, FAX

COLORADO

Colorado Historical Society
1300 Broadway
Denver, CO 80203
303-866-3395
303-866-4464, FAX

CONNECTICUT

Connecticut Historical Commission
59 South Prospect Street
Hartford, CT 06106
860-566-3005
860-566-5078, FAX

DELAWARE

Division of Historical and Cultural Affairs
Hall of Records
PO Box 1401
Dover, DE 19903
302-739-5313
302-739-6711, FAX

DISTRICT OF COLUMBIA

Department of Consumer and
    Regulatory Affairs
Historic Preservation Division
614 H Street, NW
Suite 305
Washington, DC 20001
202-727-7360
202-727-7211, FAX

FLORIDA

Division of Historical Resources
Department of State
RA Gray Building
500 South Bronough Street
Tallahassee, FL 32399-0250
904-488-1480
904-488-3353, FAX

GEORGIA

Office of Historic Preservation
57 Forsyth Street, NW
Suite 500
Atlanta, GA 30303
404-656-2840
404-651-8739, FAX

HAWAII

Department of Land and Natural
    Resources
State Historic Preservation Division
33 South King Street
6th Floor
Honolulu, HI 96813
808-587-0045
808-587-0018, FAX

IDAHO

Idaho State Historical Society
1109 Main Street, Suite 250
Boise, ID 83702-5642
208-334-3847
208-334-2775, FAX

ILLINOIS

Illinois Historic Preservation
    Agency
1 Old State Capitol Plaza
Springfield, IL 62701-1512
217-785-1153
217-524-7525, FAX

INDIANA

Department of Natural Resources
Division of Historic Preservation
Room W256
402 West Washington Street
Indianapolis, IN 46204
317-232-1646
317-232-8036, FAX

IOWA

State Historical Society of Iowa
Capitol Complex
East 6th and Locust Streets
Des Moines, IA 50319
515-281-5419
515-282-6498, FAX

KANSAS

Kansas State Historical Society
6425 Southwest 6th Avenue
Topeka, KS 66615-1099
913-272-8681
913-272-8682, FAX

KENTUCKY

Kentucky Heritage Council
300 Washington Street
Frankfort, KY 40601
502-564-7005
502-564-5820, FAX

LOUISIANA

Office of Cultural Development
Department of Culture, Recreation and
    Tourism
Division of Historic Preservation
PO Box 44247
Baton Rouge, LA 70804
504-342-8200
504-342-8173, FAX

MAINE

Maine Historic Preservation Commission
55 Capitol Street
Station 65
Augusta, ME 04333
207-287-2132
207-287-2335, FAX

MARYLAND

Department of Housing and
    Community Development
Maryland Historical Trust
100 Community Place
3rd Floor
Crownsville, MD 21032-2023
410-514-7600
410-514-7678, FAX

MASSACHUSETTS

Massachusetts Historical Commission
220 Morrissey Boulevard
Boston, MA 02125
617-727-8470
617-727-5128, FAX

MICHIGAN

Bureau of History
Department of State
717 West Allegan Street
Lansing, MI 48918
517-373-1630
517-373-0851, FAX

MINNESOTA

Minnesota Historical Society
345 Kellogg Boulevard West
St. Paul, MN 55102-1906
612-296-2747
612-296-1004, FAX

MISSISSIPPI

Mississippi Department of Archives
    and History
Division of Historic Preservation
PO Box 571
Jackson, MS 39205-0571
601-359-6940
601-359-6955, FAX

MISSOURI

State Department of Natural Resources
Division of Parks, Recreation and
    Historic Preservation
Historic Preservation Program
205 Jefferson
PO Box 176
Jefferson City, MO 65102
573-751-4422
573-751-7627, FAX

MONTANA

Montana Historical Society
1410 8th Avenue
PO Box 201202
Helena, MT 59620-1202
406-444-7715
406-444-6575, FAX

NEBRASKA

Nebraska State Historical Society
PO Box 82554
Lincoln, NE 68501
402-471-4787
402-471-3100, FAX

NEVADA

Division of Historic Preservation
    and Archaeology
100 North Stewart Street
Capitol Complex
Carson City, NV 89701-4285
702-687-6360
702-687-8311, FAX

NEW HAMPSHIRE

Division of Historical Resources
PO Box 2043
Concord, NH 03302-2043
603-271-6435
603-271-3433, FAX

NEW JERSEY

Historic Preservation Office
Department of Environmental
    Protection
401 East State Street
CN 402
Trenton, NJ 08625
609-292-2885
609-292-7695, FAX

NEW MEXICO

Historic Preservation Division
Office of Cultural Affairs
Vila Rivera
228 East Palace Avenue
Santa Fe, NM 87503
505-827-6320
505-827-6338, FAX

NEW YORK

Parks, Recreation and Historic Preservation
Agency Building 1
Empire State Plaza
Albany, NY 12238
518-474-0443
518-474-4492, FAX

NORTH CAROLINA

Division of Archives and History
Department of Cultural Resources
109 East Jones Street
Raleigh, NC 27601-2807
919-733-7305
919-733-8807, FAX

NORTH DAKOTA

State Historical Society of North Dakota
Heritage Center
612 East Boulevard Avenue
Bismarck, ND 58505
701-328-2667
701-328-3710, FAX

OHIO

Ohio Historical Society
Historic Preservation Division
567 East Hudson Street
Columbus, OH 43211-1030
614-297-2470
614-297-2496, FAX

OKLAHOMA

Oklahoma Historical Society
2100 North Lincoln Boulevard
Oklahoma City, OK 73105
405-521-2491
405-521-2492, FAX

OREGON

State Parks and Recreation
    Department
1115 Commercial Street, NE
Salem, OR 97310-1001
503-378-5001 x231
503-378-6447, FAX

PENNSYLVANIA

Pennsylvania Historical and
    Museum Commission
Bureau for Historic Preservation
PO Box 1026
Harrisburg, PA 17108
717-787-2891
717-772-0920, FAX

RHODE ISLAND

Rhode Island Historical
    Preservation Commission
Old State House
150 Benefit Street
Providence, RI 02903
401-277-2678
401-277-2968, FAX

SOUTH CAROLINA

Department of Archives
    and History
PO Box 11669
Columbia, SC 29211
803-734-8577
803-734-8820, FAX

SOUTH DAKOTA

South Dakota State Historical Society
Cultural Heritage Center
900 Governors Drive
Pierre, SD 57501
605-773-3458
605-773-6041, FAX

TENNESSEE

Department of Conservation
401 Church Street
L&C Tower, 21st Floor
Nashville, TN 37243-0435
615-532-0109
615-532-0120, FAX

TEXAS

Texas Historical Commission
PO Box 12276
Capitol Station
Austin, TX 78711-2276
512-463-6100
512-463-6095, FAX

UTAH

Utah State Historical Society
300 Rio Grande
Salt Lake City, UT 84101
801-533-3500
801-533-3503, FAX

VERMONT

Agency of Development and
    Community Affairs
Vermont Division for Historic
    Preservation
35 State Street, Drawer 33
Montpelier, VT 05633-1201
802-828-3056
802-828-3233, FAX

VIRGINIA

Department of Historic Resources
Commonwealth of Virginia
221 Governor Street
Richmond, VA 23219
804-786-3143
804-225-4261, FAX

WASHINGTON

Office of Archaeology and Historic
    Preservation
111 West 21st Avenue
KL-11
Olympia, WA 98504
360-753-4011
360-586-0250, FAX

WEST VIRGINIA

West Virginia Division of Culture
    and History
Historic Preservation Office
Cultural Center
1900 Kanawha Boulevard East
Charleston, WV 25305-0300
304-558-0220
304-558-2779, FAX

WISCONSIN

Historic Preservation Division
State Historical Society of Wisconsin
816 State Street
Madison, WI 53706
608-264-6500
608-264-6404, FAX

WYOMING

Wyoming State Historic
    Preservation Office
Barrett Building
2301 Central Avenue
4th Floor

Cheyenne, WY 82002
307-777-7697
307-777-6421, FAX

AMERICAN SOMOA

Historic Preservation Office
Department of Parks and Recreation
Government of American Samoa
Pago Pago, American Samoa 96799
011-684-699-9614
011-684-699-4427, FAX

FEDERATED STATES OF MICRONESIA

Historic Preservation Office
Federated States of Micronesia National
    Government
Division of Archives and Historic
    Preservation
Office of Administrative Services
PO Box PS 35
Palikir, Pohnpei, FSM 96941
011-691-320-2343
011-619-320-5634, FAX

KOSRAE

Historic Preservation Office
Division of History and Cultural
    Preservation
Department of Conservation and
    Development
Kosrae, FSM
East Caroline Islands 96944
011-691-370-3078
011-691-370-3003, FAX

GUAM

Historic Preservation Office
Guam Historic Preservation Office
Department of Parks and
    Recreation

PO Box 2950 Bldg. 13-8 Tiyan
Agana, Guam 96910
011-671-475-9290
011-671-477-2822, FAX

MARSHALL ISLANDS

Historic Preservation Office
Secretary of Interior and
    Outer Island Affairs
PO Box 1454
Majuro Atoll
Republic of the Marshall Islands
    96960
011-692-625-3413
011-692-625-3412, FAX

NORTHERN MARIANA ISLANDS

Historic Preservation Office
Department of Community and
    Cultural Affairs
Commonwealth of the Northern
    Mariana Islands
Saipan, MP 96950
011-670-664-2120
011-670-664-2139, FAX

PALAU

Historic Preservation Office
Chief of Cultural Affairs
Ministry of Community and
    Cultural Affairs
PO Box 100
Koror, Republic of Palau 96940
011-680-488-2489
011-680-488-2657, FAX

PUERTO RICO

Historic Preservation Office
Office of Historic Preservation
Box 82, La Fortaleza
San Juan, PR 00901
787-721-2676
787-723-0957, FAX

VIRGIN ISLANDS

Historic Preservation Office
Department of Planning and
    Natural Resources
Foster Plaza
396-1 Anna's Retreat
St Thomas, VI 00802
809-776-8605
809-774-5416, FAX

HISTORIC BRIDGE PLAQUE, SALISBURY, ENGLAND.
Nancy Welsh.

GLOSSARY

aesthetic routes. Roadways that were designed for a specific interaction with the natural or built environment. Roads for which views and details are central to their design.

alignment. The way in which a road moves across the landscape; its curves, straight sections, and hills.

arterial. A roadway providing the principal high-volume and high-speed linkages within a community and between communities.

avenue. A broad urban thoroughfare, usually tree lined.

boulevard. A broad urban thoroughfare, usually tree lined, and with a broad median.

City Beautiful. A movement at the beginning of the twentieth century focused on civic planning and aesthetic improvement. Many grand boulevards, public parks, and public buildings designed in the classical style were constructed during this period.

clear zone. The recommended area alongside a roadway clear of all potential road hazards (something a car might strike) such as trees, rocks, utility poles, and the like.

cobra-head light. The most common highway light fixture in use in the United States, so named because of the cobra shape of the fixture.

collector. A roadway providing service between arterials and local roads.

context. Refers to the setting—the surrounding area—that influences a resource such as a roadway.

cultural routes. Roadways that have evolved over time. Roads for which there is no recognized date of beginning.

designed landscape. A landscape or the alteration or modification of the natural landscape that has been created specifically to provide a certain experience to the user or benefit to the community.

design speed. The maximum safe speed at which a vehicle can be expected to operate on a roadway. The speed for which a roadway is designed (note: this may not be the posted speed).

engineered routes. Roadways that were designed for a specific transportation goal—the movement of people or goods. Roads for which the purpose of traffic movement is the principal underlying force behind their design.

errant vehicle. A vehicle leaving the roadway in a reckless or uncontrolled manner.

expectancy. A theory based on a motorist's stores of driving experiences. Routine experiences, such as sufficient merging space at the end of a freeway ramp, become unconsciously established in the driver's mind.

galvanized steel. A zinc coating applied to steel to prevent rusting. Galvanized steel has a characteristically flat, chalky gray appearance.

Green Book. The common term for the AASHTO book, *A Policy on Geometric Design of Highways and Streets.*

guardrail. A barrier, usually of a post-and-beam construction located alongside a roadway, in medians, and in front of hazards to prevent an errant vehicle from striking an obstacle or encountering a dangerous slope.

horizontal alignment. The movement of a roadway to the left or the right (its curves).

integrity. The current quality of a feature or element when compared to its original quality.

jersey barrier. An angled concrete barrier designed to guide an errant vehicle back to the roadway.

lane. A narrow passage (or road) defined by buildings, hedges, or fences.

liability. An obligation to perform a specific duty.

limited access. A concept whereby the entrances and exits of a roadway are restricted to certain locations.

local road. A roadway serving adjacent residences and businesses. A road of low-volume traffic.

median. A central space, usually planted, dividing opposite travel lanes.

National Register of Historic Places. A national listing of sites meeting the Secretary of the Interior's standards, maintained by the National Park Service.

neat line. An imaginary line representing the average face of an irregular surface, such as a stone wall.

park road. A road through a park. A park road is an element within a park.

parkway. A roadway contiguous with or linking park spaces. In its truest definition, a parkway provides access to recreational or leisure spaces.

post and cable guardrail. A guardrail constructed of regularly spaced posts connected by a flexible (usually steel) cable.

posted speed. The speed at which a roadway is signed. This is usually, though not always, lower than the design speed.

realignment. The repositioning of a roadway.

reinforced concrete. Concrete with a steel reinforcing framework. Reinforcing enables the concrete to perform in structural situations. Concrete by its nature, resists high compressive loads (the heavy weight of a truck, for example). Steel reinforcing resists high-tensile loads (the pull to the left or right one would encounter on a bridge, for example).

right-of-way. The land area associated with a roadway including all lands owned by the road management entity beyond the edge of the pavement.

shoulder. A stabilized level area adjacent and parallel to the roadway that provides a recovery space for an errant vehicle or a safe space for a disabled vehicle.

sight distance. The length of the roadway ahead that is visible to the motorist.

standards. The legally adopted policies and practices directing the design and construction of roads.

street. An urban thoroughfare, usually defined by buildings.

superelevation. The banking or sloping of a road curve to enable vehicles to maintain a speed consistent with the overall speed of the roadway.

taking. In legal terms, the direct acquisition of property, or the implementation of policies or actions that significantly impact a property (significant environmental regulations on a property preventing certain activities may be considered a taking if it is determined that the property owner is sufficiently denied the effective use of his or her property).

tort liability. A situation in which an injury or harm has occurred, due to a breach of a preexisting duty or obligation, resulting in potential exposure for damages.

traveled way. The portion of the roadway used for the movement of vehicles, not including shoulders.

vertical alignment. The movement of a roadway up and down (its hills).

volume. The number of vehicles a roadway carries. High volume is generally 1,500 ADT or higher. Low volume is less than 1,500 ADT.

Abbreviations and Acronyms

AASHTO American Association of State Highway and Transportation Officials

ADT Average Daily Traffic

Caltrans California Department of Transportation

CE Categorical Exclusion

CMP Corridor Management Plan

ConnDOT Connecticut Department of Transportation

DOE Determination of Eligibility

DOT Department of Transportation

DPW Department of Public Works

EA Environmental Assessment

EIS Environmental Impact Statement

EPA Environmental Protection Agency

FHWA Federal Highway Administration

FONSI Finding of No Significant Impact

HAER Historic American Engineering Record

ISTEA Intermodal Surface Transportation Efficiency Act of 1991

MPA Multiple Property Areas (pertains to the National Register of Historic Places)

MOA Memorandum of Agreement

MOU Memorandum of Understanding

MPO Metropolitan Planning Organization

MPS Multiple Property Submission (pertains to the National Register of Historic Places)

MRA Multiple Resource Area (pertains to the National Register of Historic Places)

MUTCD *Manual on Uniform Traffic Control Devices for Streets and Highways*

NEPA National Environmental Policy Act of 1969

NHL National Historic Landmark

NHPA National Historic Preservation Act of 1966

NHS National Highway System

NHTSA National Highway Traffic Safety Administration

NPS National Park Service

NTFHR National Task Force for Historic Roads

RIDOT Rhode Island Department of Transportation

RRR resurfacing, restoration, and rehabilitation

SHPO State Historic Preservation Officer

STURAA Surface Transportation and Uniform Relocation Assistance Act of 1987

TIP Transportation Improvement Plan

TODS tourist-oriented directional signs

TR Thematic Resource (pertains to National Register of Historic Places)

TRB Transportation Research Board

Information Sources

Federal Agencies

Advisory Council for Historic Preservation

1100 Pennsylvania Avenue, NW
Suite 809
Washington, DC 20004
202-606-8505

An independent Federal Agency, the Advisory Council on Historic Preservation is the major policy advisor to the government in the field of historic preservation.

U.S. Department of Transportation

Federal Highway Administration
400 7th Street, SW
Washington, DC 20590
202-366-4000

Federal Lands Highway
Federal Highway Administration
400 7th Street, SW
Room 4136
Washington, DC 20590
202-366-9494

Federal Lands Highway provides design and construction services for roads on federal lands in conjunction with their managing agencies: National Park Service, U.S. Forest Service, Bureau of Land Management, and Bureau of Indian Affairs.

Federal Preservation Officer
Federal Highway Administration
Office of Environment and Planning
HEP-40
400 7th Street, SW
Washington, DC 20590
202-366-2060

National Scenic Byways Program
400 7th Street, SW
Washington, DC 20590
1-800-4BYWAYS

National Highway Traffic Safety Administration
National Center for Statistics and Analysis
U.S. Department of Transportation
400 7th Street, SW
Washington, DC 20590
202-366-1537, Research
202-366-1503, Statistics and Analysis

National Park Service

National Park Service
18th and C Streets, NW
Washington, DC 20840
202-208-4621

Historic American Engineering Record
National Park Service
U.S. Department of the Interior
PO Box 37127
Washington, DC 20013-7127
202-343-4237

Historic Landscape Initiative
Heritage Preservation Services Program
Suite 200, PO Box 37127
Washington, DC 20013
202-343-9597

National Register of Historic Places
National Register, History and Education
National Park Service
U.S. Department of the Interior
Suite 250, PO Box 37127
Washington, DC 20013-7127
202-343-9536

Olmsted Center for Landscape Preservation
Frederick Law Olmsted National Historic Site
99 Warren Street
Brookline, Massachusetts 02146
617-566-1689

The Olmstead Center for Landscape Preservation is a center for landscape preservation, training, and technology development that promotes the stewardship of significant landscapes through research, planning, and sustainable preservation maintenance.

Denver Service Center
12795 West Alameda Parkway
Denver, Colorado 80225-0287
303-969-2100

The Denver Service Center houses the planning, design, and construction offices for the National Park Service.

HISTORIC ROADS ORGANIZATIONS

Historic Columbia River Highway Advisory Committee
123 NW Flanders
Portland, Oregon 97209
503-731-8234

Established by the Oregon legislature, the committee makes recommendations to the Oregon DOT and the Oregon Parks and Recreation Department regarding the preservation of the highway.

Indiana National Road Association
838 National Road, Mt. Auburn
Cambridge City, Indiana 47327
765-478-3172

The Indiana National Road Association promotes the preservation and awareness of the National Road in Indiana.

The Lincoln Highway Association
PO Box 308
Franklin Grove, Illinois 61031
815-456-3030

The Lincoln Highway Association has chapters in each of the twelve Lincoln Highway states: New York, New Jersey, Pennsylvania, Ohio, Indiana, Illinois, Iowa, Nebraska, Wyoming, Utah, Nevada, and California.

Ministerial Road Preservation Association
PO Box 651
West Kingston, Rhode Island 02892
401-783-2133

This 6.4 mile long road dates from 1668.
National Road Alliance
c/o Ohio Historic Preservation Office
Wright State University, Department of History
4th Floor, Millett Hall
Dayton, Ohio 45435
513-873-2815

The National Road Alliance addresses the preservation and recognition of the first federally funded highway in the United States. The alliance works with the historic National Road states: Maryland, Pennsylvania, West Virginia, Ohio, Indiana, and Illinois.

Historic Route 66 Federation
PO Box 423
Tujunga, California 91043-0423
818-352-7232

The National Historic Route 66 Federation is the only national nonprofit organization committed to directing the public's attention to the importance of U.S. Highway 66 in America's cultural heritage and acquiring the federal, state, and private support necessary to perserve the historic landmarks and revitalize the economies of communities along the entire 2,400-mile stretch of road.

RELATED ORGANIZATIONS

American Association of State Highway and Transportation Officials (AASHTO)
444 North Capitol Street, NW
Suite 249
Washington, DC 20001
202-624-5800

AASHTO is a nonprofit, nonpartisan association that represents the member highway and transportation departments in the fifty states, the District of Columbia, and Puerto Rico. Through its technical activities, AASHTO develops voluntary standards and guidelines which are widely used in the design, construction, maintenance, and operation of national highway and transportation facilities.

American Institute of Architects (AIA)
1735 New York Avenue, NW
Washington, DC 20006
202-626-7300

American Planning Association (APA)
1313 East 60th Street
Chicago, Illinois 60637
312-431-9100

The American Planning Association works to advance the art and science of planning, and to foster the activity of planning—physical, economic, and so-cial—at the local, regional, state, and national levels.

American Society of Civil Engineers
Committee on History and Heritage of American Civil Engineering
1015 15th Street, NW, Suite 600
Washington, DC 20005
202-789-2200

American Society of Landscape Architects (ASLA)
4401 Connecticut Avenue, NW
Washington, DC 20008
202-686-2752

The national professional society for landscape architects, ASLA also works to effect positive policies and laws at the state and federal level regarding landscape and environmental issues.

Conservation Law Foundation
62 Summer Street
Boston, Massachusetts 02110
617-350-0990

The Conservation Law Foundation works to solve the environmental prob-lems that threaten the people, national resources, and communities of New England.

National Scenic Byways Clearinghouse
1440 New York Avenue, NW, Suite 202
Washington, DC 20005
1-800-4BYWAYS

The National Scenic Byways Clearinghouse is a library and reference center established to serve as a central source of information on scenic byway programs and issues. Copies of corridor management plans and other road management documents are available to the public. The Clearinghouse is a joint project of FHWA and the American Automobile Association.

National Task Force for Historic Roads (NTFHR)
National Trust for Historic Preservation
1785 Massachusetts Avenue, NW
Washington, DC 20036
202-588-6279

The National Task Force for Historic Roads is housed within the Rural Heritage Program of the National Trust for Historic Preservation. The purpose of the NTFHR is to promote the recognition of historic roads and routes of historic significance and to advocate the protection of their integrity of design, purpose, and use.

National Trust for Historic Preservation
1785 Massachusetts Avenue, NW
Washington, DC 20036
202-588-6000

Established by Congress in 1949 as the nation's historic preservation advocate, the National Trust works to provide leadership and technical assistance in all areas of historic preservation. It maintains regional offices in Boston; Charleston, South Carolina; Chicago; Denver; Fort Worth; and San Francisco.

Scenic America
21 Dupont Circle, NW
Washington, DC 20036
202-833-4300

Scenic America is a nonprofit organization whose mission is to preserve and enhance the scenic character of America's communities and countryside. In particular, the organization works to fight visual blight such as billboards and commercial strip proliferation.

Society for Commercial Archaeology
PO Box 2423
Atlanta, Georgia 30301-2423

The oldest national organization devoted to the commercial built environment. The organization works to preserve, document, and celebrate the
structures and architecture of the twentieth century: diners, highways, gas
stations, bus stations, neon lighting, and more.

Surface Transportation Policy Project (STPP)
1400 16th Street, NW
Suite 300
Washington, DC 20036
202-939-3470

STPP, a private, nonprofit organization, works to ensure that transportation
policy and investments help conserve energy, protect environmental and
aesthetic quality, strengthen the economy, promote social equity, and make
communities more livable.

Texas Transportation Institute
801 CE/TTI Building
College Station, Texas 77843
409-845-1711

The Texas Transportation Institute conducts highway research and is the nation's principal facility conducting crash tests.

Transportation Research Board (TRB)
2001 Wisconsin Avenue, NW
Washington, DC 20007
202-334-2933

The Transportation Research Board is a unit of the National Research
Council, which serves as an independent advisor to the federal government
on scientific and technical issues of national importance. TRB conducts research concerning the nature and performance of transportation systems.

REFERENCES

GENERAL REFERENCE

Conservation Law Foundation, *Take Back Your Streets,* Boston: CLF, May 1995.

Hewes, Laurence Isley, *American Highway Practice*, 2 volumes, New York: John Wiley and Sons, Inc., 1942.

K. L. Hancock, A. G. Hansen, and J. B. Mayer Jr., *Aesthetic Bridge Rails, Transitions and Terminals for Park Roads and Parkways*, Federal Highway Administration, FHWA-RD-90-052, Washington, DC, 1990.

Minnesota Department of Transportation, *Aesthetic Guidelines for Bridge Design*, St. Paul: Minnesota Department of Transportation, Office of Bridges and Structures, 1995.

National Park Service, Denver Service Center, *Road Character Guidelines, Sequoia and Kings Canyon National Parks*, Denver, Colorado: National Park Service, 1990.

National Research Council, Transportation Research Board, *Location, Selection, and Maintenance of Highway Traffic Barriers*, Washington, DC: National Research Council, National Cooperative Highway Research Program Report No. 118, 1971.

National Research Council, Transportation Research Board, *Designing Safer Roads: Practices for Resurfacing, Restoration, and Rehabilitation*, Washington, DC: TRB Special Report 214.

National Research Council, Transportation Research Board, *Transportation Aesthetics*, Washington, DC: Transportation Research Record No. 1549, 1996.

Rypkema, Donald D., *The Economics of Historic Preservation*, Washington, DC: National Trust for Historic Preservation, 1994.

Sensible Transportation Options for People (STOP), *Traffic Calming: The Solution to Urban Traffic and a New Vision for Neighborhood Livability*, Tigard, Oregon: STOP, 1993.

U.S. Department of Transportation, Federal Highway Administration, *Summary Report on Aesthetic Bridge Rails and Guardrails*, FHWA-SA-91-051, Washington, DC, 1992.

Wick, Jim, *A State Highway Project in Your Town? Your Role and Rights: A Primer for Citizens and Public Officials*, Burlington, Vermont: Preservation Trust of Vermont, 1995.

History and General Interest

Billington, David P., *The Tower and the Bridge, The New Art of Structural Engineering,* New York: Basic Books, Inc., Publishers, 1983.

Coates, Ken, *North to Alaska! Fifty Years on the World's Most Remarkable Highway*, Toronto: McClelland and Stewart, Inc., 1992.

Hokanson, Drake, *The Lincoln Highway: Main Street Across America*, Iowa City, Iowa: University of Iowa Press, 1988.

Least Heat–Moon, William, *Blue Highways, A Journey Into America*, Boston: Houghton Mifflin, 1982.

Raitz, Karl, ed., *The National Road*, Baltimore: Johns Hopkins University Press, 1996.

Raitz, Karl, ed., *A Guide to the National Road*, Baltimore: Johns Hopkins University Press, 1996.

Steinbeck, John, *Travels with Charley*, New York: Penguin, 1962.

Wallis, Michael, *Route 66, The Mother Road*, New York: St. Martins Press, 1990.

INDEX

ADM-5503

6/2/98

TE
23
M37
1998